The Education of Gypsy and Traveller Children

towards inclusion and educational achievement

The Education of Gypsy and Traveller Children

towards inclusion and educational achievement

Christine O'Hanlon and
Pat Holmes

Trentham Books
Stoke on Trent, UK and Sterling, USA

Trentham Books Limited

Westview House	22883 Quicksilver Drive
734 London Road	Sterling
Oakhill	VA 20166-2012
Stoke on Trent	USA
Staffordshire	
England ST4 5NP	

First published 2004

British Library Cataloguing-in-Publication Data
A catalogue record for this book is available from the British Library

1 85856 269 4

Designed and typeset by Trentham Print Design Ltd., Chester and printed in Great Britain by The Cromwell Press Ltd., Wiltshire.

Contents

Christine O'Hanlon is an Honorary Reader in Education at the Centre for Applied Research, University of East Anglia. She is a teacher educator who uses action research to assist the professional development of teachers and educational professionals so that they can make learning successful for a wide range of pupils through investigation and change in their working contexts. She teaches courses aimed at widening participation and access in educational contexts for pupils who are marginalised or otherwise seen to be outside the mainstream of traditional schooling practices. She is the author of *What is your school doing for Travelling children?* a staff development pack for the European Federation for the Education of the Children of the Occupational Travellers (EFECOT, 1996).

Pat Holmes has worked with Gypsy and Traveller children in a variety of educational capacities. Since 1986 she has been managing the West Midlands Consortium Education Service for Travelling Children (WMCESTC), a regional, education and field welfare support service, on behalf of the fourteen local education authorities in the region. In 1980 she set up the National Association of Teachers of Travellers (NATT). As a result of her collaboration with Ludo Knaepkens, NATT became a founder member of the European Federation for the Education of the Children of Occupational Travellers (EFECOT) in 1988, of which she is past President and currently Vice President. She has contributed to several books and publications on issues concerning education for Traveller children.

Preface

The purpose of this book is to draw on the lifestyles and experiences of Traveller communities to highlight their presence in our schools and classrooms or their absence from educational processes and to outline the subsequent implications for meeting their educational needs. It aims to provide information and support to head teachers, LEA and Traveller Education Support Service (TESS) advisers and teachers in preparation and provision for the inclusion of Traveller children in their schools.

The book is the result of collaboration between Christine O'Hanlon, and Pat Holmes the Principal Adviser and Co-ordinator of the West Midlands Consortium Education Service for Travelling Children (WMCESTC). They constructed and ran a twelve month course consisting of three modules, partly taught and part distance learning, through the process of action research. It focused on advancing the educational progress of Traveller children and was an accredited part of the post graduate Education programme based at Birmingham University. We thank Trish McDonald, Senior Adviser (Teaching and Learning) WMCESTC for her help on the course.

Those who attended were managers and advisory support teachers from twelve English local education authorities TESS. This book is dedicated to the course participants and their commitment to using action research to help them to support colleagues in addressing some of the practical and attitudinal obstacles that prevent or delay inclusion and educational progress of Traveller children in schools. Contributors to the case stories include: Nicola Redwood, Eirlys Cleaves, Anthea Wormington, Kathleen Cresswell, Sheila Keighley, Sue Todd and Stephen Wray.

1
Travellers, who are they?

This book is about the education of Traveller children. Education is a process we normally expect to progress from the early years to 16 years in a school environment, yet there are children, who because of lifestyle and cultural factors cannot access schooling contexts easily and for whom schooling is an intermittent and often difficult route to navigate. We begin with some important definitions and distinctions related to Traveller communities in the UK.

The term Traveller suggests an homogenous group of people and immediately misinforms us. There is no one single group of Travellers. Traveller is a collective term for all those ethnic minority, business, professional and cultural communities who travel for work purposes or who keep travel as an option and key reference point in their lives even when they are settled.

In their own communities the families may assert their specific identities as: Gypsy (English, Welsh), Traveller (Irish, Scottish), Showmen (Fairground) and Circus. These are the traditional communities in the United Kingdom today.

*   Gypsies and Irish Travellers are minority ethnic communities protected by the 1976 Race Relations Act.

*   Showmen are a business and cultural community who, by their organisation around a single business interest for generations

I

and with a history of planned movement, are distinctive from the other Traveller communities.

- Circus families, both British and international, also travel for work purposes around a single business interest and are just as distinctive by virtue of their lifestyle, professional structure and organisation.

- there remains a small group of families travelling and working as carriers on the Canal networks in the UK. Their number has been increased by settled families seeking to live and travel on narrow boats, as canals open up for leisure purposes. They work, permanently or seasonally, retaining occupations they had while living in a house.

In the 1980s and 1990s New Age or New Travellers emerged. They were mainly young people and young families from settled, white mainstream culture who adopted a Traveller lifestyle for their own reasons. Some were educated young people who made the choice for environmental, anti-materialistic reasons, opting out of the rat race. Others were escaping the negative cycle of homelessness, family conflict or breakdown. Their travel is often limited to the seasonal festival tours, otherwise they show a preference for more permanent stopping places where they can live the new lifestyle.

It was in response to the mass gatherings and raves of the New Travellers in the 1980s that the government of the day, who saw them as subversive and anti-social, introduced legislation to curb their activities, which in turn impacted critically on Gypsies and Travellers (Public Order Act 1987).

In the 1990s and the early years of the new millennium to date, Roma (Gypsies) from Eastern European countries began to arrive as refugees and asylum seekers. Denied their ethnicity and the freedom to pursue traditional work under communism, they had been forcibly settled and drafted into agricultural cooperatives and factories. After the fall of communism market forces in the states led to acute un-employment levels. The Roma were the first to be forced out. The new nationalism gave rise to scapegoating, victimisation, violence and even murder of Roma by local populations, including neo-nazis. Although the national governments all state an allegiance to equality in law, in practice little appears to be done to stop the discrimination and hostility practiced locally against the Roma.

Brief Histories

Gypsies

There is significant evidence to indicate that Gypsies first migrated into Britain from Northern India in the early 1500s. UK inhabitants at the time thought they were Egyptians on a pilgrimage because of their dark skin and different language. They were originally given safe passage by the king on this basis. This belief led to the settled population calling them Gypsies (derived from Egyptian).

Gypsies use a language known as Romani. Scholars believe that the Romani language is derived from Sanskrit (Prakrit). It is a spoken language although there have been efforts to establish an agreed written international Romani in order to promote and reclaim the language. Hindi and Punjabi speakers will recognise a good deal of shared vocabulary with Romani:

pani – water	dikked – saw
penned – said	chal – son
vel – welcome	mush – man
delled – gave	chavi – child
latchered – found	drom – road
rooker – tree	sutti – asleep
dadrus – father	lovva – money
tan – place	Yog – fire
dai – mother	
kushti – good	(Acton et al 2000)

Romani is more widely in use in mainland Europe where Roma populations are greater than in the UK. After generations of erosion as a result of rejection and inter marriage in the UK, it remains in use today mainly as an Anglo-Romani dialect, described as poggerdi jib – literally, *broken tongue*, with greater or lesser use of vocabulary or phrases depending on the experience and commitment of families to transfer the language from generation to generation. After the fifteenth century, their failure to leave the country, their language, traditions, values, work interests and nomadic lifestyle led them to be more and more marginalized, stigmatised and penalised as strangers. By the sixteenth century it was a capital offence to be a Gypsy, a situation not repealed until the mid 1800s.

Today Gypsies are still disadvantaged because legislation fails to provide sites for Travellers to stay on, preventing or impeding their access to mainstream services and facilities. It is believed that over 30 per cent of the community still have no legal place to stay and many people continue to feel justified in excluding and discriminating against the Gypsy community at an institutional and personal level. Some people seem quite willing to blame and stereotype the entire community for the actions of the few. Newspaper reports and signs on the doors of some public houses continue to damn and exclude Gypsies without any real fear of redress by the law, despite the 1976 Race Relations Act and the Amendment Act of 2000.

Racist reporting and signs saying 'No Travellers' should be referred to the Commission for Racial Equality (CRE) for action but the level of media and public hostility towards Travellers remains largely unchallenged and ignored at a formal level.

Gypsies' former work patterns and interests were to operate as extended families, providing mobile workforces as seasonal labour, knife and tool grinders, hawkers and traders in homemade goods and horses. After World War Two increased car production and rapidly extending road networks as well as the mechanisation of farming and improvements in manufactured goods, led to the decline of traditional work.

New legislation accelerated the adaptations that had to be made in seeking new work opportunities, for example, the 1959 Highway Act made it an offence for Gypsies to camp on road verges. The Caravan Sites and Control of Development Act (1960) made it an offence for anyone to allow their land to be used as a caravan site without a licence from the local authority. It set minimum standards for facilities and maintenance. Most farmers and landowners could not or would not provide these facilities for families they no longer needed in large numbers and, faced with prosecution, were forced to evict hundreds of Gypsies onto the road.

Traditional stopping places now lost are occasionally remembered only by names of streets or lanes such as Gypsy Lane and Romany Way. The families had to move on and seek new work opportunities, some of which no longer lent themselves to whole family activities. Often it was heavy labour that was demanded, although some families continued with their traditional work, for example, working as a family to sort and clean metals for recycling.

There was impetus to further diversify into, for example, selling furniture and carpets and other areas where dealing and selling skills could be pursued without formal education and schooling.

Irish Travellers
Irish Travellers have a much more obscure and perhaps older history than Gypsies. There are known to have been indigenous nomadic smiths making and mending pots and pans in the Middle Ages in Ireland. Their language, Gammon, also known as Cant, is believed to have also been spoken by those from the old religion who were cast out when Christianity came to Ireland (Macalister, 1937). Today an Anglo-Gammon dialect remains, stronger in some families than others. For example, *the gallya is lush-ing alamach* translates as the child is drinking the milk (Binchy, 2000).

Some scholars believe the population of Travellers was swelled by communities dispossessed of their homes and land during the famine in the nineteenth century.

There is recorded evidence of Irish Travellers in England in the 1800s but it was Ireland's attempts in 1963 to bring in policy to settle families in houses, against the wishes of Travellers, that led to large numbers leaving Ireland. The majority came to Britain and thus increased the travelling population in the UK.

Families were attracted to urban areas where scrap collecting and tarmacing in particular, provided key work opportunities. They became much more visible to local communities as they camped in urban areas, largely without legal places to stay. Irish Travellers experienced and continue to experience significant levels of rejection and discrimination for being Irish as well as for being Travellers.

Competing for scarce work opportunities, and incompatibilities related to differences in lifestyle, has sometimes resulted in suspicion and inter-group rivalry between Gypsies and Irish Travellers. This situation is often exploited by the press and local politicians in terms of who are the 'real Gypsies' and, by implication, the more deserving, and who are the imposters and undeserving.

In truth, both communities have much in common as nomadic groups although their historical roots are different. They share a history of travelling for work purposes. They have both traditionally operated outside the mainstream wage labour system as extended family mobile workforces. They have child-rearing practices which support and teach their children as trainee adults to be inducted into the family work tradition as mature workers at 12 or 13 years of age. Family education is strong and effective and predominantly promoted through visual and kinaesthetic learning styles, that is through seeing and doing.

Both communities have a strong tradition which puts family loyalty above all else. Children are reared for their place in the family and traditionally family takes precedence over the individual. In this way families have transferred culture, values, beliefs, practices and work skills from generation to generation, to ensure continuity of and adherence to the culture.

Both communities have a good eye for, and commitment to, symbols of wealth which can be readily converted to cash when needed. Some of these include gold jewellery, good china and glassware and state of the art trailers, vehicles and cars.

Gypsies traditional belief systems have, for many Gypsies, given way to the organisation of the Gypsy Evangelical Church and many families travel to attend Gypsy churches and follow mobile missions around the country from Easter time into summer.

Many families travel to mainland Europe for religious events including Saintes Maries de la Mer, near the Camargue in France, where thousands of European Gypsies gather twice yearly to revere the Black Virgin as their patron saint, the statue of which is in the local church.

Irish Travellers are largely and traditionally Roman Catholic. The importance of their children's induction into the Church and religion is stressed by parents. Many families still seek only Roman Catholic school places for their children. Families may ensure new trailers are consecrated by the priest and, for example, during November for the feast of All Hallowes, whole families will gather at the graves of loved ones either in England or in Ireland, to ensure their religious duties are carried out.

Gypsies generally adhere to hygiene practices rooted in Hindu laws of cleanliness. Some of the traditions and beliefs in many families have changed – for example a menstruating woman is considered spiritually unclean (*mochadi*) and should not handle food – but many other beliefs and practices are still intact. The most modern and well equipped trailers still do not have toilets or showers in them because of beliefs in cleanliness and the safeguarding of family health by keeping spiritual uncleanliness outside the home.

Clean water is still poured from closed cans and a range of bowls are still used to separate different washing activities such as food, clothes and person. There is no evidence to support Irish Travellers having roots in concepts of spiritual cleanliness, nevertheless many have also adopted practices akin to Gypsies in an attempt to preserve the health of the family.

Both Gypsies and Irish Travellers engage in increasingly varied work as traditional options disappear. Furniture, carpet dealing, skip hire, roadmaking, tarmacing, garden clearance, trailer, car and land dealing, tree lopping, landscaping, roofing, and antique dealing are all areas where Gypsies and Travellers seek a living. Increasingly, families travel to other countries for months at a time, to pursue work in mainland european countries like Germany, Spain and Portugal.

However, with rapid economic changes, new technological demands and expansion of the service industries, unqualified and uneducated workers find earning a living is becoming more and more difficult.

A small handful of families still live in horse drawn wagons (*vardos*) carved and highly decorated. Heavy distinctive stainless steel embossed trailers are still valued by some families. Inside, abundant glass and mirrors reflect light and space. Engraved and bevelled glass emulates traditional designs from the wooden carved *vardo*.

Today, families prefer to purchase modern continental trailers from mainland Europe, indistinguishable externally from mainstream quality caravans on the road, but still retaining the observances of no bathroom or toilet. Space is at a premium and families observe finely planned use of space and operation within the trailer. Family education has served the community effectively in previous generations but now many are expressing the need to add new skills to existing ones if they are to survive in the future.

The needs of young adults in the community, many of whom have no family work to be inducted into, and no formal skills to transfer into new work opportunities, are critical. They have not inherited the world of their grandparents' and parents' experiences and many are involved in some generational conflict as a result of the demands of the future and the demands of the traditions, culture and expectations of the parent and grandparent group. Traveller communities are attempting to find a new balance in order to survive as independent and confident people.

Gypsy and Traveller Populations

It is not possible to be accurate about the size of the Gypsy and Traveller population in the UK because there has never been a formally conducted census. In 1965 in England and Wales a census was commissioned but this was carried out by the police and was inaccurately low. Although the then National Gypsy Council challenged the results and offered additional information, the exercise was neither credible nor conclusive. Gypsies and Travellers are not included as categories in the national census. Every study and report makes its claim for population size although each rightly points out that numbers are likely to be greater because of the added difficulty in counting those families who have been long settled in houses. One source cites eighty thousand (Liegeois, 1998) while more recently it is claimed that there are one hundred and twenty thousand (Kenrick and Clark, 1995).

Gypsy and Traveller Representation

Representation and self advocacy for Gypsies and Travellers has been fraught with historical conflict, the remnants of which still exist today. A number of organisations have been established to represent their human rights. One of these, the Gypsy Council was set up in 1966, but internal differences about the way forward led to a series of political splits in the 1970s. Subsequently three groups were formed from the split. One group formed the National Gypsy Education Council (NGEC) a combination of academics and professionals and Gypsies, another became the Advisory Committee for the Education of Romany and other Travellers (ACERT) which had a similar make up of membership. The small Romany Guild also collaborated with ACERT. The third group left from the Gypsy Council was rebranded as the National Gypsy Council (NGC) with a commitment to ensuring that Gypsies should be in charge of their own affairs, with support from non-Gypsies only when requested. The main commitment of the organisation was to securing accommodation for Travellers but they also sought quality health care and integration with support within mainstream education. These organisations still remain active today.

However, in recent years the NGEC has become the Gypsy Council for Education, Culture, Welfare and Civil Rights (GCECWCR) but promotes itself as The Gypsy Council. The National Gypsy Council reverted to The Gypsy Council saying that Gypsies and local and county officials always refer to it in this way. ACERT continues as a support organisation.

In addition, other groups have emerged to support specific groups within Traveller communities, or to support Gypsies and Travellers in general.

The ideological conflict and struggle for a unified voice continues to indicate the different values and cultures represented within the broad terms of Gypsy and Traveller. The struggle is replicated at some level across other countries in Europe and demonstrates the distance still to go to establish self-advocacy and representation in communities who have no history or tradition of political or collective organisation.

Further professional developments have occurred recently through the formation of the Birmingham based Traveller Advice Team (TAT) at the Community Law Partnership representing Gypsies and Travellers countrywide mainly on accommodation issues. The team publish a regular newsletter on their activities. Cardiff Law School, in collaboration with TAT and other support organisations, has drafted the Traveller Law Reform Bill calling for equality in accommodation, education, health and educational opportunities for Travellers. Though the Bill is unlikely to find its way onto the statute book, because it has been introduced as a ten minute rule Bill it is hoped that some clauses might be positively incorporated into other legislation presently passing through parliament.

Showmen (Fairground)

The Showmen or Fairground community have a long history from Roman times of providing entertainment at markets, trade and hiring fairs and seasonal festivals across the land.

From the middle ages until as late as the early twentieth century, hiring or mop fairs were held where workers were put up for hire and wore a 'mop' or symbol of their trade in their lapels so that everyone could see what skills there were to hire. For example, Stratford Mop in Stratford on Avon was granted a Charter in 1196, and still operates as an entertainment fair today.

The use of steam in industrial contexts led in 1868 to the first steam roundabout. It was invented by Savage in Norfolk and this moved the fair from muscle powered rides to greater sophistication characterised by the galloping horses (gallopers) accompanied by mechanical organ music. The fairs were the first to bring electric light and moving picture shows to a wider public.

The dates of the historical Statute and Charter fairs are still adhered to today despite the ever changing economic and social climate. The modern fairs still bring entertainment to the public on specific dates at different venues in the UK.

The Van Dwellers Association (now The Showmen's Guild of Great Britain) was established in 1889 to protect and organise Showmen around the business of the fair. It has strong structures and rules and regulations which all members must comply with. The Guild has ten regional Sections: London and Home Counties; Eastern; Western; Midland; South Wales and Northern Ireland; Nottingham and Derby; Yorkshire; Lancashire; Northern and Scottish.

Each Section Committee includes an Education Liaison Officer who liaises with parents, Traveller Education Support Services (TESS), schools, local education authority officers and other interested parties. There are an estimated twenty-one to twenty-five thousand travelling Showpeople in Britain (Kenrick and Clark, 1995). There are also smaller organisations of mainly part-time showmen.

The World's Fair is an independent weekly trade paper which carries trade, social, professional and historical features of interest to the Show and Circus communities. Traditionally the first fair on the Showmen's calendar is King's Lynn, Norfolk in February, although nowadays Leeds Valentine Fair has proved successful and a number of city new year extravaganzas include a fair.

The family living wagons are large with pull out sections providing or extending rooms. Wagons have toilets and bathroom, living room and bedrooms.

The wagons are high off the ground and are reached by stairs leading up to a covered porch. Family living space may be supplemented by providing independent space for older children in a tourer caravan parked nearby. The wagons can be plugged into mains electricity on the winter site and operated by generator whilst travelling.

The majority of Showmen pull out of their winter yards for the touring season at the end of March or earlier. They used to return mid October after the 'back end run', but the advent of bonfire fairs has extended the season and pull in is usually November. Whilst out touring, families who have the same winter yards may not see each other until they return to the home yard.

The lessee (boss) of the fair negotiates and rents a location for the fair from local authorities or private land owners. He is responsible for the smooth running of the fair. There are rules and regulations covering safety and environmental health and also the interests of each member. A fair does not move as one outfit to each new loca-tion. Individual or groups of rides are booked for each occasion. Some families have established routes and contracts developed over generations, whilst others work hard to plan and fill their season with regular work and a viable route. Some families travel within one locality or region within a season, whilst others travel widely throughout the country. The ground is planned and build up is precise with safety issues of paramount importance.

The fair usually opens at 5 or 6 pm and closes around 10.00 pm. Clearing and covering up will add at least another hour to the Showmen's day. Pulling down before moving on is an equally precisely planned operation. Fairs may operate for one day, a few days, a week or maybe two weeks at big traditional events such as Nottingham Goose Fair, Hull Fair, Newcastle 'Town Moor' Fair, St Giles Fair Oxford, Cambridge Midsummer Fair, Warwick Mop, and Stratford Mop.

Showmen are increasingly seeking to extend their work opportunities to compensate for the higher costs of new sophisticated equipment and the upkeep and costs of operating as Showmen. After pulling back into winter yards at the end of the season, some families may be part of contracts which ship equipment abroad for winter work in Hong Kong, Singapore and Dubai for example, or they may be repairing and restoring their rides and then pursuing other family business interests or seeking other winter work opportunities as drivers or salespeople.

It is this time of the year when weddings and other social and community events will be held or families take holidays. Sometimes families will briefly pull out again for a Christmas fair and families will try and maintain a regular market or sports event with their ride or catering stand. The extended season and search for venues abroad all indicate the efforts to maintain and, where possible, enhance working opportunities.

Children are introduced into family work from a young age, by being with and learning from parents as they work and in being encouraged to help where they can. Children are inducted into the business at an early age. Guild rules reinforce the national legislation in terms of child employment.

There is a strong tradition of transferring skills to children to support the family business. Families hope that their children will remain in the business, work to maintain it and later inherit it.

There is still a strong tradition of encouraging young people to marry within the community to reinforce the skills and workforce needed for the continuity and perpetuation of the business.

UK Showmen believe that they are born Showmen but the competing developments of new entertainment and theme parks are creating new challenges for them. It is becoming the practice in mainland Europe for fairgrounds to be seen as business opportunities with positions going to the highest bidder. There are also specific qualifications and legal requirements to becoming a Showman currently being discussed and planned in Europe alongside general planning of work profiles. These are all strong reminders to the Fairground and Showmen's community of increasing competition and regulation in a fast changing world.

The National Fairground Archive is located at Sheffield University under the Directorship of Dr Vanessa Toulmin, who is a member of a Showmen's family.

Circus

Philip Astley, a sergeant major in the English cavalry, introduced circus in London in 1768 as a trick rider. He subsequently worked to introduce circus across Europe.

At the beginning of the 19th century many European cities had a permanent circus as well as travelling shows and circus. In 1820, tents were introduced along with admission charges rather than voluntary collections being taken within the watching crowd. Circus increased its repertoire to include a whole range of human skills, from clowning to wild animal acts. In 1929 in the USA, multi-ring circus was introduced by the Barnum and Bailey and the Ringling Brothers' circus. It was the largest circus on the move and used 300 tents to stage a show.

Today in the UK there are nineteen circuses travelling, mostly seasonally and some for eleven months of the year. There are large circuses with contracted acts as well as small family circuses. There is traditional circus and circus with new skills shows.

Families teach skills generation to generation. Some new circuses in the UK and on mainland Europe have schools with attached funding in order to teach and accredit circus skills. Permanent circus schools operate in France, Belgium, Germany and the UK. The debate and reflection of British and International circus is reported in the *World's Fair* weekly newspaper.

Circus proprietors have the Association of Circus Proprietors (ACP) to protect and promote their interests. Parents have established the Circus Parents Association (CPA) to promote the need for improving the educational opportunities of their children.

In the 1980s there were four mobile circus schools. A report on these schools by her Majesty's Inspectorate of Schools (HMI, 1988/89) concluded that the provision had numerous difficulties which needed to be addressed if they were to continue and become more effective. Recommendations were comprehensively detailed in order for 'substantial improvements to be made in the quality of the pro-vision', which to date have not been addressed.

Currently there are no mobile schools in the UK although the CPA are urging the Department for Education and Skills (DfES) to return to, and address, the HMI recommendations, or alternatively to develop new technologies as a way of addressing the distance learn-ing education of secondary aged children in particular, during the travelling season.

Circus is both British and international. Often English needs to be taught as an additional language to young circus people when they travel in the UK and enter local schools.

A variety of caravans are used by Circus families, including some with pull out sections, which are built to be pulled by articulated cab. Most families return to winter quarters for the winter months. Chil-dren return to and attend their local school where their places would have been kept open for them under dual registration legislation.

2

Community values and experience: their implications for early years, primary and secondary schools

Historically school is the institution of another culture, established for the sedentary population. Schools' efforts to accommodate and respond to increasingly changing and diverse populations are well documented and reflected in government policy and legislation, DfES and Ofsted reports.

The open door policy of the 1950s and 1960s, where schools were there if you wanted them, failed Gypsy and Traveller children miserably. There are many adults in the Traveller community who testify to the prejudice, hostility and rejection they experienced in schools at this time, if indeed they managed to overcome the barriers to access school at all.

It was not until the government began to introduce broader funding and regulations to support LEAs in the 1980s and 1990s to provide education and welfare outreach services to families and support to schools, that Gypsy and Traveller children began to take up schooling.

In the early stages attempted registration at school was often met with hostility and rejection. There was an obvious mismatch between school and the mobility of families, but the hostility was not based on the organisational challenges presented, as many of the families were settled locally, but on prejudice against Gypsies and Travellers as people.

Other parents withdrew their children from school because they didn't want them mixing with Gypsies. Some parents picketed schools or education offices waving banners of rejection.

If the children did manage to register, some schools insisted that they were taught separately away from the rest of the school community. This also meant different start and end times to the day, different break times and different areas to play in.

Other arrangements were organisationally the same. Provision was away from the rest of the school community, even in units on Traveller sites or via visiting teachers. This provision had a different ethos however, seeking to give children their first opportunity to develop some reading, writing and school behaviour skills before eventually joining mainstream classes. There were debates about whether separate provision enabled children to develop confidence, competence and self esteem in learning, or whether it served to compound their social exclusion and marginalisation.

Only one segregated provision that we are aware of was closed, having succeeded in its stated task of preparing and transferring children into mainstream classes with support (Worcestershire, 2001). The final report to the LEA was quietly triumphant.

For the most part, such provision became the only provision and was only phased out as a result of increasing awareness with regard to equality of educational opportunity, the development of multi cultural education practices and government legislation and funding programmes which were increasingly aimed at 'ensuring unhindered access to and full integration in mainstream education' (DES Circular 10/90).

Nationally it has taken over twenty years to establish the current educational opportunities for Gypsy and Traveller children. Many schools have had particular difficulties in welcoming and making meaningful provision for them. As the Swann report states: 'In many ways the situation of Traveller children in Britain today throws into stark relief many of the factors which influence the education of children from other ethnic minority groups – racism and discrimination, myths, stereotyping and misinformation, the inappropriateness and inflexibility of the education system and the need for better links between homes and schools, teachers and parents' (Swann Report, 1985).

Traveller and Gypsy children perceive the home as the primary learning environment. They enjoy a great deal of freedom in the area outside the trailer where they can explore and play and work hard. Coming into the trailer is a much more finely disciplined affair.

Children are expected to observe the trailer as a relaxing space to sit, eat and talk. Many homes have expensive china, glassware and ornaments around and in glass cabinets. Young and old respect the inside space.

Space is at a premium however, in terms of bringing up a family in a trailer. Storage is for essentials.

The children are used to adult attention. They learn alongside the adults by watching and copying and being allowed to make mistakes on the way to developing skills.

They are also used to learning within mixed age groups that will include a range of extended family members as well as siblings. They are engaged in work and care activities all focused on the family interests. On reaching puberty children will no longer be treated as children because they are seen to be mature.

Children will be aware of any struggle in the home about the status of education and whether they will be supported into school or not. Often the choice of whether a child goes to school is ostensibly left to the child by the parents. This is unique in a situation where children are traditionally expected to do and act as parents require in the interests of the family. It is often an excuse for parents' own disagreement or anxieties regarding education waving their responsibility for their children's attendance at school.

Outreach workers to families, through for example TESS, need to be aware of the implications of these issues for the child entering school and to be sensitive but clear in supporting parents to support their children.

Names

Many Gypsy and Traveller families name their children within the historical and cultural framework of the community as practised in many other cultures. Within the Irish Traveller community, any of the clan surnames within a family may be used interchangeably depending on the status of the name in an area.

They generally baptise their first born boy after paternal grandfather (grandaddy) and the first born girl after grandmother (grandmammy). In a large extended family this means that there may be several young people named, for example, Patrick and Kathleen. However, children will be given family names which seem to people outside the culture to be informal nicknames. For example:

Girls	Boys
Tadey	Flickey
Korky	Cricket
Wawa	Tudey

Many children will be given a baptismal name and a family name. Children and parents should be asked what name they want to use in school.

Gypsy children may historically have names that have been in the family for generations and are recognised as family names. For example:

Girls	Boys
Serefina	Crimea
Miracle	Darcus
Granny Girl	Jim Boy
Mizzelli	Reuben

Family Learning

All Traveller families have a tradition of learning together. Schools as institutions are not organised in this way but some parents will still expect and hope for family grouping in schools. Organising children chronologically in classrooms often perplexes families and leads to their requesting family education in line with home traditions. Older siblings will be expected by parents to care for younger ones at school and they will have to answer to parents for the child's well being at the end of each day. It is helpful if schools initially support older siblings in fulfilling family expectations. Anxieties may be lessened if siblings can:

• help younger children settle in, particularly if they are distressed

• have checking out arrangements, just until children have settled

• know the times in the day when they can see each other and be together so the older child can relax and concentrate on their own school experiences.

Dates of birth still do not have the same significance for Traveller families as for the literate bureaucratic organisations of the settled community but they are becoming increasingly important as families become more involved and engaged with national recording systems. Mothers can sometimes adapt the age of a child to favour a place in the primary setting rather than in a secondary school. This is not so much deliberate deceit but more a mother seeking what she perceives as the best, most secure child centred environment for her child. Support to overcome those fears and anxieties is necessary if parents are to be persuaded that a secondary school can provide the best setting for their children's needs.

Traveller families are not dominated by time in the same way as the settled community. For many families, it is still daylight hours which dictate to families the length of a day's work. Traveller families, without access to amenities, don't take for granted modern facilities in homes, like light and heat at the flick of a switch. Days of the week, months, time in a day, may all be approximate for families who are governed by the event, the immediate, rather than by pre-arranged timetables and deadlines.

Establishing the habit of school attendance for some children re-quires involvement with the parents and older siblings to de-liberately build into the family day the school start and finish times. It is often useful and necessary to support the habit by providing transport in the initial stages.

Days in the week when, for example, physical education or cookery equipment are needed, will require initial prompting. Reminders may need to be built in until pupils are familiar with their timetable and what should be brought to school in association with particular lessons each day.

Space in the family trailer is extremely limited and storage of special equipment for school is not always a priority. Teachers can help Traveller children by providing a safe space in school for key equipment. Homework requirements are not easily met in a caravan or trailer. Not only is storage space at a premium, so too is space for doing school work. Nor will Traveller children be likely to have someone to understand and support them with homework, because their families have no school experience and because of the low priority of school work and the ethos of home. Children may often experience negative peer pressure regarding homework responsibilities. Teachers will need to consider ways in which children can be supported in completing homework on school premises, or with outreach support in the home, so that Traveller children don't miss out in learning and are actively assisted in achieving school related tasks. Many schools have homework clubs for children who wish to use them. Traveller children need specific support to be fully included in school work through homework management. Good liaison with parents is important to explain why children are required to work after school hours and the benefits that accrue from it.

Implications for schools
Early years
Traditionally younger children in Gypsy and Traveller homes have had the benefit of care within the extended family. Grandmothers, mother, aunties, cousins and all siblings older than the child have had care responsibilities. Childcare was the family responsibility and pride.

The youngest child's family status was often extended until they were six or seven years old because of parents' reluctance to allow the child to begin formal education at statutory school age. Once parents allowed children to go to school they were often at a disadvantage from having missed so much of structured early learning experiences in reception classes.

Social and economic change over the last decade or so, combined with outreach work of the TESS and the greater national focus on early years opportunities, has meant more Gypsy and Traveller children are engaged in play and nursery settings.

The increased fragmentation of the extended family as a result of changing accommodation and work circumstances has meant, for the first time, many nuclear families are managing childcare and making a living for themselves or in different contexts from the extended family.

Sometimes children brought up on a local authority site have had no place to go on reaching adulthood or marrying. Local policies regarding accommodation for Travellers do not extend in practice to planning and preparing for natural community growth. Subsequently some young families find themselves on other sites or on the road and, in terms of the extended family, on their own. Those on the road without a legal place to stay often do not have the skills of their grandparents and parents for managing life while constantly on the move and frequently experiencing eviction. Families in both situations often require support for their children in terms of play and nursery provision. Some parents living on sites are aware of their geographical isolation from local amenities and communities and see places in local playgroups or nurseries as a supplementary experience to what they can provide on site for their child.

This growing awareness may be prompted by a young mother's own positive experiences of primary education and a developing perspective of the need for formal education in the life of her child. Isolated families with no local facilities have become more responsive to using the loan system for structured playboxes promoted by local TESS, or to visiting mobile play facilities.

Although there are the Sure Start nationally funded initiatives to address disadvantage among three to five year olds in localised areas, they have been geographically based, so excluded the children who were not in specific project areas. Where the area has included Traveller families, many initiatives have been imaginative, creative and inclusive and they have been able to work closely with the local TESS. Many LEA Early Years and Childcare Development Partnerships have also increased awareness and responsiveness to the needs of young Traveller children through their work with TESS.

Picture books, story sacks and other early learning resources reflecting young Traveller children's lives and interests have been developed. Playgrounds on site, transport and escort support, additional project staffing, support with fees and mobile outreach playbuses in isolated rural areas, are just some of the responses to the developing partnership between providers and parents in creating access to early learning opportunities for Gypsy and Traveller children. This has made a significant impact on successful and smooth transfer from playgroup and nursery to school at statutory school age.

There is a long way to go but, as first educators of their children, increasingly Gypsy and Traveller mothers are choosing to place their children in early years settings. There appears to be a developing awareness and confidence in what early years providers are extending to their children.

It remains invariably mothers who voice their wishes for their children to have early years opportunities and who have some belief in education providing new opportunities for their children for the future. Traveller fathers are generally more conservative about the prospect of outside influences being brought into the home, although there are many exceptions. They fear erosion of the tradition of passing on the culture from generation to generation in order to ensure the continuity of the way of life. This can lead to strong differences of opinion in the home and a struggle to establish take up of early years or school provision. Primarily seen as the main carer of the children, women can be viewed with concern and anxiety by their husbands for apparently wanting to relinquish this role to outside providers (see early years case study chapter 6).

Primary School

Many teachers who want to construct good quality provision have been hampered not only by pre-conceived ideas of the Gypsy and Traveller communities but also by lack of information and support. Assumptions have been made that whether Traveller children are five or nine years old when entering school for the first time, they must know something, as we do, about structure, practice, and routine of the school as an organisation. However, it is important not to assume anything about a Traveller child's experience, but ensure a thorough induction is put in place that creates genuine access to the school and its curriculum to welcome every new child.

School language and practices such as separation by age mentioned earlier, routines and procedures such as lunchtime, queuing, sitting and eating at a table, will need to be deliberately taught so that children are given every opportunity to understand what is expected of them to perform well and succeed in the classroom and school.

It is important to give attention to the support the child might need in the early stages for activities in the classroom, in the unstructured and informal areas of the day and in other parts of the school. Particular attention is needed to ensure that children who have not had access to flush toilets and hot water on tap are taught how to use them properly and safely.

The size of the school building may equate with outside space for many Traveller children. They may not have been in such a large building before or remained in one by themselves for any length of time. Teachers may need to be particularly aware of those children for whom operating inside a building proves physically very difficult at first. Because of spacious school rooms children cannot use their existing home knowledge in the same way. Induction and support need to reinforce the purpose of each space in the building and identify appropriate activities for each location as well as provide support for children to achieve this. To begin with, teachers might limit the child's working space in the classroom for short periods of time in order to support and encourage concentration skills and focus on desk based activities until they become familiar and confident in operating in different kinds of space in the school.

Children may wish to cling to the indoors because it is structured and safe, rather than go out at play or lunchtime. Many schools recognise that various children require a sanctuary area in school during these times. Provision and staffing of such an area reduces much of the difficulty that can occur during break times and subsequently spill over into class.

Because their lifestyle often leads to a late start and intermittent interrupted attendance, Traveller children often have significant gaps in learning. This is most in evidence in terms of their literacy when initial assessments are made in school. Teachers can view children as having learning difficulties rather than having lacked the opportunity to learn. Assessment and misplacement in class may be potentially damaging to the child, other children and the teacher if the child's responses, experiences and skills are not appropriately assessed and responded to from an informed position. Traveller children's learning and school potential is difficult to assess within the prescriptive framework of the National Curriculum or Standard Assessment Tests. Schools may wish to draw on the support of the TESS to assist and advise on initial assessment.

For children who have not had consistent formal learning opportunities, the provision of accelerating programmes rather than slow learning approaches may prove more rewarding. Using the knowledge of children's home learning styles and linking children with good learning models will be more productive than treating them as having special educational needs and placing them with children with learning or behavioural difficulties. Giving the Traveller child multiple learning opportunities and having high expectations for their achievement will motivate and encourage their success in school.

When children fail to make progress, investigation will be needed into the cause: gaps in knowledge or a specific learning difficulty. Appropriate and speedy responses are required to support Traveller children diagnosed with learning difficulties particularly where children still travel with their families and need the safety net of professional assessment to guide other schools and LEAs in meeting their needs.

When trying to establish the habit of regular attendance, it is important not to use exclusion as a disciplinary sanction. Exclusion gives the wrong signals to Traveller children and parents about the importance of attendance. Alternative disciplinary or classroom management strategies are required for children who are learning to settle into new school routines and who can misbehave when they read the cues wrongly. Many schools, which routinely teach Traveller children, are able to communicate differentiated responses when managing behaviour and can transmit the message to pupils that while consistency is vital, it does not mean one size fits all. An inflexible behaviour management policy can undermine the efforts of a school and related services in supporting parents and children when prioritising good attendance.

Although Gypsy and Traveller children predominantly speak English, the style and construction of their speech, plus the use of Anglo Romani or Anglo Gammon, can cause communication difficulties in school. Many children are operating exclusively within their specific language community when they are not at school (see case story on *Traveller language in school?* in chapter 6). If the child's accent, dialect or delivery is difficult to understand, it is equally important when engaging children in conversation, that they receive the message that there is value and interest in what they are saying. Slowing them down, asking for other words to help, and demonstrating interest in the content of the exchange overrides any temporary or intermittent comprehension difficulties. Listening and communicating clearly is important for all concerned in a learning situation.

Traveller children may be puzzled by language style, for example when a request may seem like a question such as, 'Would you like to hang up your coat?' which implies choice, when in reality it is an instruction.

We need to be aware of our own language use and check that Traveller children have understood what we expect them to hear, particularly in relation to instructions. When they attend school regularly however, children learn the language of school and its particular social interaction, and how it differs from what they are accustomed to in their own community. Schools concerned at Traveller children's lack of school language need to be cautious not to dismiss children's language capabilities within their own community, family and work experience. Teachers need to have it acknowledged that they are teaching additional language skills to supplement those the children already bring with them to school. Encouraging the use of home language in oral or written work in a natural and non-threatening way also demonstrates to children the value placed on what they have to say.

Teachers need to understand the cultural differences of Traveller communities, particularly for example, when they encounter

Traveller children's resistance to physical education. Most often it is not the activity children shy away from, but the immodesty of the changing and showering facilities and the perceived inappropriateness of clothing for the activity. With sensitive management children can be accommodated and enabled to enjoy physical education (PE). Modesty codes remain strong in Traveller communities and these values should be respected in schools.

Using curriculum and resource materials in the classroom and library which positively reflect Gypsy and Traveller communities have enormous impact on children's self-esteem and motivation. In addition, learning projects which use Traveller materials, demonstrating their way of life and portraying Travellers positively to the rest of the school community, raise whole school awareness constructively. This contributes to a good learning and social environment for all pupils and especially Traveller pupils.

TESS may loan resources to schools initially but it is better if schools purchase their own materials so that they are not seen as external, bolt on or temporary but as part of the school's operational everyday resources. Artefacts can be loaned from TESS. Drawing on Traveller experience in the curriculum wherever possible will help to engage and motivate those Traveller pupils who may feel alienated or disaffected. Children who operate in learning institutions where there is no reflection of themselves or their experience can rightly believe that they are invisible, with all the implications that can have for their self identity, self esteem and social image.

Teachers who observe Traveller children gathering together in the playground may view it as gang like behaviour. However, social group gathering is normal for initial security, familiarity and solidarity with friends and family in an unfamiliar environment. When sensitive, constructive and supportive school action is taken teachers can lend understanding, value and status to the Traveller group. Importantly they can encourage other school relationships based on collaborative working and shared responsibilities such as, becoming a monitor, sharing classroom and playground games and roles, developing working partnerships. This gives opportunities for children to interact in a structured way and to find out about each other in a non-threatening situation. This is particularly important for Traveller children who may be short-term registrations and who will have few opportunities to develop and build friendships with other children. They may find it difficult to become accepted in an already socially established classroom or school network. Deliberately finding ways of valuing short-term relationships provides opportunities for all children to extend their understanding to a wider range of peers.

Children from Fairground, Showmen's and Circus communities have difficulty attending school for periods of the year because their touring calendar and the school calendar are not complementary. Strategies for addressing their needs are detailed in Chapter 3.

The following ckecklist of good practice is a quick and accessible route to confirming provision already in place and identifying actions or resources needed to support improving provision in schools and classrooms:

Good Practice Checklist – Primary

- Welcome at Reception:
  - speedy admission
  - positive clear expectations
  - sensitive help with form filling where necessary
  - sensitive explanation of ethnic categories and purpose
- Establish positive collaboration with TESS
- Identify designated staff member for Traveller support
- Develop home/school liaison
- Follow up previous pupil education records with parents (*Red Book*), TESS, previous school records and work examples
- Arrange children's induction through buddying for example (providing good role models), shadowing, induction, and mentoring
- Establish regular whole staff professional development on cultural awareness, and inclusion strategies, for example,
  - create active and transparent equality and behaviour policies and practices
  - use appropriate assessment procedures to identify gaps in learning, and the strengths and needs of children
- Make arrangements for the speedy referral of Traveller children with learning difficulties
- Establish target setting, support input, review of curriculum progress and attainment

- Put regular data monitoring in place to identify pupil underachievement
- Ensure the reflection of Traveller culture in teaching and learning curriculum, curriculum materials and resources
- Identify support necessary and possible with TESS
- Establish effective attendance monitoring and follow up
- Avoid exclusion as a sanction while seeking to establish attendance patterns
- Make sensitive arrangements for physical education, changing and showering
- Provide a sanctuary area particularly for the unstructured times of the day
- Provide homework support
- Put system in place for providing and managing distance learning work for seasonally travelling children in school who are unable to register in schools as they travel because of rapid movement. This needs to include planning meetings with parents preparing to travel, and welcome back meetings to review and reward pupil's distance learning work achievement.
- Put system in place to support transfer preparation of Traveller children away from school base during summer term
- Arrange outreach support to encourage inclusion of parents in school events, open days and so forth
- Plan for sensitive communication systems with parents recognising the inappropriateness of written material
- Implement sensitive management and inclusion of short stay children
- Ensure senior staff support in raising teachers' expectations regarding Traveller children's potential.

Secondary Schools

Gypsy and Traveller children are at extreme risk of failing to transfer to secondary school and many choose to absent themselves. Ofsted comments:

> Access to the curriculum for secondary aged children remains a matter of grave concern. There are possibly as many as 10,000 children at this phase who are not even registered with a school (*The Education of Travelling Children*, Ofsted 1996).

While many Traveller parents value primary education for its child centred approach and attention to the teaching of reading and writing, education at the secondary phase challenges traditional and cultural beliefs and practices which are right at the heart of the family.

It was formerly thought that when Gypsy and Traveller children were firmly established in primary education, particularly those children on local sites and yards with security of base and definable travel patterns, the habit of attendance would, with careful preparation, transfer successfully from the primary to the secondary phase. This is true for some children who benefit from good planning, family support and commitment, and a good home-school relationship. However, for many families, the struggle for secondary education for their children is still in a process of negotiation.

Firstly, families, despite the economic and social changes which challenge their traditional concept of family, see their young people who are post puberty as mature adults, and expect them to take on adult working roles within the family. Young people who go to school often have to endure enormous negative peer pressure from Traveller young people who avoid school to fulfil their traditional destinies. This will happen even when there is no obvious family work for many of them to be engaged in.

The moral code of conduct within many families is strict. Girls are not generally allowed to mix with the opposite sex after puberty without the presence of parents or older brothers. Many children are still matched for marriage in order to enhance and strengthen the economic and social ties between extended family groups, and ensure cultural and traditional continuity.

Secondary schooling is seen by many parents as a threat to their cultural and moral codes and practices. Fears of boy and girl contact, sex and drugs education, whether in the curriculum or playground, all conspire towards parents seeing secondary schooling as a potentially eroding influence on their young peoples' commitment to the continuing traditions and way of life. Parents try hard to keep their children away from influences which may otherwise educate or attract them away from the values and practices of the family and the community.

Additionally, parents see secondary schools as dangerous places in terms of racist bullying both within the school and on the way to and from school. Placing their young people in such an environment, where they are vulnerable is seen as a dereliction of parental duty by many parents. The seeming irrelevance of much of the curriculum concerns all parents whether their children are in secondary education or not. In general, Gypsy and Travellers feel no one listens to them or their children about their hopes and needs for their perspectives on the future.

While Traveller families were viable as mobile workforces inducting children early into the workforce, the boys working apprentice style alongside the men, and the girls providing the childcare and domestic support alongside the women, there was no need for formal education skills. However, the quiet social and economic revolution is rapidly bringing into sharp relief differences in generational experiences and outlook.

The need for the extended family as a mobile labour force has largely gone with the demise of core industries and, with it, most of the traditional Traveller work opportunities. Exposure to television, video, shops, and schools means that many of the younger generation are not protected from modern external influences and no longer isolated within their own communities. Families who remain economically, socially and culturally confident struggle with these issues, often despite their personal security, but young people from less fortunate situations feel bewildered at the failure of their families to provide. They feel isolated, and sometimes resentful, at the affluence and opportunity they witness around them. Many Traveller young people increasingly demonstrate that they are just as vulnerable as other young people in society by succumbing to crime, promiscuity, drugs, and alcohol.

Although many young Gypsies and Travellers retain traditional aspirations of owning a motor and trailer, being married, having a family and being self employed, they are hoping for new opportunities. The characteristic of the community over generations has been its ability to adapt to changing economic circumstances. Parents must afford their children support in taking up secondary education because new school opportunities can compensate for the absence of traditional ones that have been lost. However, parents need to have evidence and the confidence that schools will play their part in a genuine and transparent partnership in order to change their belief in schools as institutions of assimilation rather than places of social inclusion and pluralism. At present children and young people are caught up in a struggle between the tensions and influences of home and school.

When they support their children, Traveller parents will also be supporting the continuity of their culture by ensuring their young people are sufficiently capable and skilled and thus confident enough to assert their cultural confidence in school contexts. However, the quest to find a better or a more economically stable life should not necessarily compromise community distinctiveness and difference As Anisha states:

> The components which hinder harmonious integration are not necessarily cultural but rather economic. Being integrated into society can only provide more strength to affirm our true and human values. The majority population is not 'a-cultured' (loss of culture) because they have a bathroom, electricity, medical care and universities (WMCESTC, Partnership Project, 1997).

Inclusion of Traveller children and young people at school is essential to their affirmation and social acceptance. Schools must genuinely enable Traveller access and approval that depends upon a flexible and adaptable use of the school curriculum. Secondary schools need to strive to adopt a genuine and transparent partnership approach. Where there are only one or two Traveller children in the school, it is difficult for them to assert their identity without feeling exposed and vulnerable, but where there are groups of them, their confidence together as a distinctive group can be interpreted as challenging and disruptive by schools that do not understand the invisibility and marginalisation they feel in institutions which don't recognise or respect them. All parents and young people need to have confidence that school will be welcoming, informed and responsive to their needs if they are to make the best of their opportunities there.

It is an indictment of our society that for the most part Gypsy and Traveller children who have succeeded in school and adult learning have done so mainly by denying their identity and presenting as members in the mainstream community, for fear of hostility, prejudice and rejection. This denial is the result of consistent emotional, social and psychological degradation. It denies positive role models to other Gypsies and Travellers in the community and continues the myth that Gypsies do not and cannot achieve in secondary schooling and beyond.

The requirements of schools as public institutions to promote good race relations under the Race Relations (Amendment) Act 2000, will help schools in their efforts to build or extend a genuine transparent partnership. Schools are required to have an efficient Race Equality Policy, report racist incidents and monitor and report the performance of minority ethnic communities and to assess and take action on underachievement. Since January 2003, Gypsy, Roma and Travellers of Irish heritage, have been included in the DfES ethnic categories for schools and LEAs. While there is a great deal of evidence that many families were frightened, reluctant and unwilling to expose themselves formally by ascribing to a Gypsy or Traveller ethnicity for fear of rejection, it is only positive school and LEA actions on their behalf that will give parents confidence to ascribe to their real identities, heritage and way of life.

The new and expanding opportunities at secondary level, at Key Stage 3 and new strategies for 14 to 19 year olds, will assist schools in responding more practically to Traveller needs and aspirations. More vocational options in the curriculum, partnerships with colleges and other providers, work experience opportunities and access to Personal Advisers from the Connexions Service all lend themselves to attracting young people to hitherto narrow academic institutions. Schools will need to demonstrate a proactive stance by putting their students first and ensuring that resources will support a relevant curriculum for young Travellers.

There are many examples of good and improving practice in secondary schools for social inclusion and the development of relevant curriculum, but they are not yet the wider norm in all schools.

Some of the challenges posed by the needs of Gypsy and Traveller children, reflect the experience of many other children from minority ethnic groups and individuals for whom secondary school seems an alien and hurtful experience. However, Gypsies and Travellers as a community are largely absent from the secondary curriculum and school process, therefore addressing their needs is urgent if we are not to lose another generation from secondary education. Young Travellers will be introduced to, and experience, the very best of both worlds if parents are involved in a genuine and transparent school partnership with mutual interest in bringing young people into a dynamic and supportive educational atmosphere. Traveller experiences and skills gained through the strength of family education is an additional skill potential for secondary school education to enhance all student's future lives. Ofsted agrees:

> All successful work securing regular attendance and confident and successful learning was directly linked to the quality of the relationship with the parents (Ofsted, 2001).

A genuine and transparent partnership is one which is honest in recognising the power dynamics of the relationship between home and school. Parents know that the school represents mainstream culture and that it challenges the traditional organisation of their community. Many see it as an instrument of social control. Education is a legal responsibility which some parents see as enforced assimilation. On this basis, some parents will move on, send their young people to relatives or choose home education in the safe knowledge that they will not be traced. They realise that in the main no one is interested, organised or resourced sufficiently to check, monitor and track each young Traveller throughout their school lives. Families become invisible to the system. Young people become stranded from formal educational opportunities.

For parents to work beyond this and to effectively support their young people in secondary education, they will need to experience a routine demonstration of good practice by schools towards building a relevant education for their young people in an active partnership with themselves as parents. The mutual parent-school dependency needs to be acknowledged, recognising that the contribution of each is weakened in the absence of the other. This partnership is capable of narrowing the gap between home and school for the child and enhancing young Travellers' future life chances. Failure to enter into the partnership by either party will leave another generation of young Gypsies and Travellers with unrealised personal and economic potential.

The following checklist of good practice is a quick and accessible route to confirming provision already in place and identifying actions or resources needed to improve provision in schools and classrooms:

Good Practice Checklist – Secondary

- Welcome at reception
    - speedy admission
    - positive clear expectations
    - sensitive help with form filling where necessary
    - sensitive explanation of ethnic categories and purpose
- positive collaboration with TESS
- a designated staff member
- a home/school liaison plan
- previous pupil education records with parents (*Red Book*), TESS, previous school followed up
- pupil induction, buddying (providing good role models): shadowing, induction, mentoring
- whole staff professional development of cultural awareness, inclusion strategies
- prior identification of support needed and possible with TESS
- active and transparent equality and behaviour policies and practices
- appropriate assessment procedures and instruments to identify gaps in learning, strengths, needs of child
- speedy referral of Traveller children with learning difficulties
- target setting, support input, review
- data monitoring in place to identify underachievement
- reflection of Traveller culture in teaching and learning curriculum, curriculum materials and resources
- effective attendance monitoring and follow up
- avoidance of exclusion as a sanction whilst seeking to establish attendance patterns
- sensitive arrangements for physical education, changing and showering that do not offend
- sex education with sensitive outreach to parents to seek support and co-operation
- provision of sanctuary area particularly for the unstructured times of the day
- sensitive management and inclusion of short stay children
- senior staff to raise expectations of teachers regarding Traveller children's potential.
- agree with Educational Welfare Officers, parents, TESS, pupils, appropriate learning packages for Traveller pupils new to schooling or with significant limited primary experience and unable, initially, to access the secondary curriculum

- support for Traveller pupils fourteen years old and above in accessing vocational courses and learning through other providers as appropriate, to encourage continuing learning and prevent disaffection and dropout.

- homework support

- system in place to support transfer preparation of Traveller children who will be away from school base during summer term

- strategies in place for transfer, and dealing with implications for seasonally travelling children joining the school after the start of the academic year

- system in place for providing and managing distance learning work for seasonally travelling children in school who are unable to register in schools as they travel because of rapid movement, including planning meeting with parents preparing to travel, and welcome back meeting to review and reward distance learning work achievement.

- outreach support to encourage inclusion of parents in school events, open days etc

- sensitive communication systems with parents recognising the inappropriateness of some written material

3

Supporting mobility: educational continuity strategies

Keeping Records

Good record keeping is important for all children but particularly for children who are mobile for all or part of the year and who experience interrupted education. Records are an essential continuity strategy in the education of travelling children.

While there is no legal requirement for schools to write records for children with less than four weeks stay in the school, it is precisely these children who most need and benefit from a formal account of their learning experiences and achievements. Schools, with the capacity to see themselves as part of a network of schools which will provide education for children as they travel, will undertake record writing, not only to assist the child and the next school, but to reflect the values of the school itself as serious and accountable educators.

For short stay children, two kinds of records can be made available to the school.

For Gypsy and Traveller children who are highly mobile, without a home base and base school to return to from travelling, many TESS provide Short Stay Records for schools to complete, often with the assistance of their own advisers and/or support teacher from TESS working in the school.

In the case of seasonally travelling children, such as the primary circus child who enters new schools regularly during their touring period, they will be carrying the National Parent Held Record of Education Development Book known as *The Red Book* (NATT/ DfES).

Targets, learning experience and progress need to be recorded in the book while the child is at the school and handed back in the little red bag to the child or parents as they leave. This Parent Held Record works well and effectively demonstrates the importance and strength of parent/teacher relationships.

Transport

Where Gypsy and Traveller families without a legal place to stay are subject to regular eviction over short distances, transport provision is a useful continuity strategy in enabling children to continue attending the school in which they were first registered in the area. This provides a degree of stability amid the turbulence of unplanned movement by the family but importantly a period of stability in which children can embrace school and learning.

Some sites are geographically isolated from local amenities and some journeys between home and school are hazardous. Transport is a useful access and continuity strategy in helping to establish and maintain attendance of children from these situations. Some TESS have transport budgets to assist children but LEA's can also decide to provide where necessary.

Traveller Education Support Services TESS

The TESS is potentially an important partner and resource for a school. The outreach family liaison role, which is the cornerstone of the TESS work, will ensure that the gap between home and school can be positively reduced towards parents and schools becoming direct partners with a diminishing but supportive role for the TESS.

The TESS will always play an ongoing key support role in relation to families without a legal place to stay and those who are highly mobile. Schools will require advice and support from TESS for short stay pupils. In relation to seasonally travelling children, the TESS may initiate and support the schools preparation of distance learning work and the school's partnership with parents in organising their children's work for the touring season. It is the TESS around the country who will activate visiting teachers to teach and monitor distance learning work, or arrange school places for children according to their tour itineraries. TESS will also support parents and schools in arranging for national tests and exams to be taken in other school locations as families travel, if parents are too far at a distance to return children to base school.

The size and shape of TESS varies across the country according to resources available and the importance placed by LEAs on bringing the children of the most marginalised communities into the school process.

All TESS focus on deployment of resources and strategies to support LEAs, schools and Education Welfare Services to address access, attendance, continuity and achievement for travelling children (5-16 years).

TESS will also be engaged in linking 3-5 year olds and post 16 students with providers, or may have special initiatives within the team to support these areas of education for Traveller children and young people.

TESS also offer a range of services to schools which includes:

- home-school liaison
- whole school Inset delivery and professional development particularly regarding cultural awareness
- inset/professional development to key groups of staff including new staff
- advisory skills focused on policies and practice for the inclusion of Traveller children
- curriculum development, adaptation and differentiation
- support for distance learning work development and management
- teaching and learning materials and in particular culture specific material for short term loan. In schools regularly registering Traveller children, TESS resource catalogues will enable schools to purchase resources themselves

- induction support for new pupils
- support for assessment and record transfer
- classroom assistant support
- direct partnership teaching to accelerate learning with groups or occasionally with individuals short term, backed by a School Support Agreement which focuses on targets, shared input by TESS and school and review
- support to class teachers to differentiate gaps in learning because of interrupted schooling, and learning difficulties as a result of learning interference or special educational needs

TESS will support schools and local education welfare services in establishing good working practices regarding the admission and attendance of Traveller children. TESS will also work within inter-agency contexts linking families with key professionals as requested or where necessary.

Transfer

Many Traveller children are travelling away from school when preparation for secondary transfer takes place in primary schools and it is therefore important to ensure all formal procedures for transfer have been completed before families begin to travel. Early signs of risk of failure or reluctance to complete transfer forms need to be followed up.

There is no standard preparation to support successful transfer and systems range from minimum to excellent practice from school to school.

Most schools' preparation for transfer will include at minimum an introductory visit to the secondary school in the final term of Year 6. Other schools however have developed a range of strategies including teacher exchanges between primary and secondary during Year 6, where children have opportunities to work within a curriculum area such as Information Technology at the secondary school during the final term. Other successful techniques include a buddying system of linking Year 6 pupils with secondary pupils for induction and shadowing visits, visits to parents by year heads and perhaps the pastoral head, and open days and evenings for the potential new intake.

Schools can call on their local TESS to assist where children will be away travelling during important exchanges with the secondary school. Earlier links can be negotiated to ensure transfer provision so as to familiarise Traveller children with the new environment they will be returning to after the travelling period.

For children in Year 6 who are travelling with distance learning work, there is an opportunity to provide experience of secondary school through collaboration between primary, secondary and TESS to ensure the work reflects some of the Year 7 curriculum. This can support and provide opportunities to explore some of the language of new secondary subject areas, acquaint Traveller children with their teachers, and familiarise them as much as possible with the school. Distance learning work needs to be marked and assessed by Year 7 teachers who have set the work, or a designated person in the school, to ensure continuity of children's learning between distance learning and return to school.

Transfer Checklist
- intervention and action in advance of transfer
- support to parents in their choice of school
- use of *Are We Missing Out* (DfES, 2001) video for parents
- nurture group for children at risk of not transferring
- raising expectations of secondary schooling with children and parents
- making visits (earlier arrangements to be made if children will not be at school when the Year group plans have been scheduled)
- teacher primary-secondary planning and communication
- buddying and shadow arrangements for induction
- opportunities for working experience at secondary school
- distance learning arrangements in place
- good record keeping documenting children's strengths and needs
- school awareness of, and contacts with, TESS for assistance where necessary

It may be more productive for children who have had little primary education or who are newly joining a school at the secondary phase pre-transfer, to stage entry, with support, and steadily build up to full access and attendance. This enables the child to develop their learning confidence and self-esteem and enables the school to ensure appropriate responses and provision are in place for children, particularly those who may need additional learning, language or reading support. A package or plan arrangement needs to be supported by Education Welfare Service, LEA officers, school, pupil, parents and TESS.

Arrangements for national tests and examinations

Returning children to base school, or arranging assessments in a school on their tour, are the main continuity strategies to include children in national assessments.

While it is currently a hit or miss affair for highly mobile children without a structured travel route to access national tests, teacher assessments are crucial for Traveller children's school success. For children with planned routes, many parents try to bring their children back to base schools for national tests, or where children are socially and academically confident, some parents will ask the base school or TESS to organise for the child to take tests in a school close to where they will be on their tour. There is a heavy reliance on teacher assessments where families are not able to do either, but, increasingly, schools and TESS engaged in a strong partnership with parents are demonstrating children's involvement in national tests and examinations despite movement.

Parents have confidence in teacher assessments outside the national examination structure i.e GCSE, NVQ's, but they are increasingly seeking ways to improve children's access to national formal accreditation and require DfES to recognise their need for greater flexibility and innovation for access and delivery so that mobile children can have equality in terms of participation and achievement in national examinations.

School based distance learning work

For seasonally travelling children (including Fairground and Circus children) who move too rapidly to enter school as they travel, school based distance learning work, developed by the school and TESS, provides their curriculum for this period. The work is normally supervised by parents and has regular teaching and support visits from the national network of TESS staff in the LEAs wherever families are stopping.

Distance learning work is not a legal requirement on schools but is encouraged by DfES as a good practice strategy in maintaining children's contact with class work as they travel. According to Ofsted (2001):

> Action on Traveller Education at the national level should ensure that there is more systematic development and use of distance learning material.

Local schools attended by seasonally travelling children, which children will return to each winter when they return to their home base at the end of the touring season, are called base schools. Children remain on the school roll as they travel and schools mark the register as authorised absence whilst the children are travelling.

School based distance learning can vary in content, quality and presentation. Some schools are committed to well differentiated and presented work in order to support and motivate children. Particular care is taken to provide prompts and guidance for self study pupils. Most of the work prepared is still paper based, with some video or tape support, although the potential for support via the new technologies is already being explored through European Community funded project work and CD Rom support.

Innovations continue to be developed. For example, in one region, Secondary Schools have formed a distance learning network in partnership with TESS in order to share responsibility for writing the school based distance learning (SBDL) work provided for their secondary students who travel.

In addition, a loan system of laptops enables children's presentation of their work to improve and also allows for e-mailing work to and from the base school or TESS tutor. It is anticipated that more sophisticated provision such as the successful in pilot projects organised by EFECOT, and working on line with tutor support, will be established more widely.

Currently schools make individual arrangements with parents about how new and completed work can be exchanged between them during the travelling season. In *What is Your School Doing for Travelling Children? a guide to equal opportunities through Distance Learning* (WMCESTC/EFECOT, 1993), the features of school based distance learning are introduced through a series of inter-related sections which show that effective support means a partnership between teachers, parents and students. The partnership should ensure the following:

- relationship with the client group to be the first priority in all work undertaken, especially in identifying the kind of materials required

- children to be taught self study skills and techniques in order to take some responsibility for their own work while travelling

- wherever possible, pupils to be supported by personal contact with teachers and peripatetic (TESS) staff whilst travelling.

- materials must be appropriate for the level of support the children are expected to receive

The importance of the parental partnership and the joint planning process is highlighted in Chapter 4 of *Fighting Social Exclusion through ODL* (Holmes *et al*, 2000).

The Staff Development Guide *What is Your School Doing for Travelling Children?* (O'Hanlon, 1996) is written as reflective action research guide which assumes that learning takes place with active professional investigation and planning for teaching and learning. It aims to provide a process model for staff to:

- individualise learning for students

- consider equal opportunity issues in the context of learners at a distance from school

- improve the quality of teaching and student learning

- try out new methods of teaching

- develop new strategies for organisation and management

- develop creative strategies for the production of new materials

Children from Fairground, Showmen's and Circus communities have difficulty attending school for periods of the year because the touring calendar and the school calendar do not match. As families prepare to leave for the touring season in March, schools will normally meet with them and a representative from the local TESS to discuss the school based distance learning work the children should take with them. This work is based on the national curriculum and follows the expected work that the class would be following in their absence. The school and TESS co-operate together to ensure that the work is appropriately differentiated and organised to facilitate self study by fairground pupils. The mechanism for returning and collecting work in the following months is agreed with individual families or groups, and arrangements are made to keep in touch. Some schools arrange exchange of postcards to keep children in social contact with friends and staff in the school.

Where families have a ready planned itinerary, TESS can arrange visiting teacher support as the family travels. *The Education Contact Book* (NATT/DfES) can be used by parents to telephone ahead and arrange for visiting teacher support from TESS. If parents are standing in only one or two places for the season they can use the contacts book to ask TESS to arrange places for the children in a local school. Whenever families are in their local area, their children can attend their local or base school.

Arrangements for national assessments and exams need to be made in advance to ensure that parents bring children back to the base school or for TESS to arrange for children to take tests in another school in the area they will be in. The TESS would provide educational support for the child.

For secondary aged pupils, travelling has more serious implications. The exam syllabus at their base school may not necessarily be the same as in other secondary schools, consequently, distance learning work is vital. However, visiting teachers from TESS cannot be subject specialists across the whole secondary curriculum, which is unsatisfactory for young people who need teaching and where minor learning problems and difficulties need to be addressed before they become major problems. It is essential that other strategies and solutions are identified to meet their needs.

Recording progress and setting targets for pupils as they travel in the season is important. It helps motivate and focus children. This can be done in the provided Record Book from the winter base school or TESS, or in the National *Red Book*.

Access to national assessments and examinations can all take place while the family is travelling. Schools can plan for transfer preparation and induction and options can be chosen before the child leaves for the season. Additionally, Year 6 distance learning work needs to be set by year 7 teachers to ensure that children are prepared for the move to secondary schooling. Otherwise their late start at the secondary school may result in an entire absence from the class work from September to November.

When children return to school in November, many schools hold a welcome back meeting or, at secondary level, a review meeting. This is where children can be acknowledged and rewarded for the completion and quality of their distance learning work while curriculum plans are made for their successful inclusion in new classes with new teachers.

Some sections of the Showmen's Guild award vouchers to children whose teachers' assessments of their distance learning work is good. They do this to acknowledge and reward the child for achievements in self study with limited professional support, to recognise parents commitments to their children's learning and to demonstrate that the community increasingly values their children's achievements within the formal learning process.

Teaching support for children as they travel still remains patchy across the country and is dependent upon different resource levels of the TESS in particular areas. Some Circus families travel eleven months of the year and cannot always spend the twelfth month in the same winter quarters and therefore have no base school. It is the children of these families who are acutely excluded from the education planning process. The resource pack *Circus Spotlight* (NATT) is designed to support schools and classes in learning more about circus life.

Because of the extended touring season, many children do not achieve 100 days attendance at school. The DfES currently do not feel they can grant 'off site' status for distance learning work, although they strongly encourage schools to provide the work.

In turn schools feel unfairly disadvantaged because despite providing and managing distance learning work, in partnership with

TESS, they must mark the travelling children as 'authorised absence' in the register, which in turn depresses the schools attendance profile. They also feel Ofsted do not take any interest in this aspect of the attendance profile during inspections, but are really only interested in, and report on, the overall attendance profile for the school. Therefore, it doesn't always give a balanced attendance profile for the school. As a result schools feel penalised despite their efforts to support Showmen's and Circus children.

NATT is currently researching across TESS the number of individual pupils annually touring and how many visiting teacher support visits pupils receive during a travelling season. This is in order to plot the level of professional support and tuition being received whilst touring and to assist further debate on the issue and impact of distance learning as a valid continuity strategy. It is hoped that in future distance learning can become an off site activity and offer appropriate levels of professional support and tuition to pupils as they travel. If school based distance learning is to be an effective continuity strategy it is important that:

- record systems are in place, in active operation and understood by all parties

- there are adequate staff, time, resources and materials to support effective and motivating distance learning

- work is differentiated according to individual pupils' needs

- children are taught self study skills so they can take some responsibility for their own learning whilst travelling, and that systems to support them are built in to the work

- teacher training and staff development is provided

- the distance learning work provided has its roots in the classroom curriculum and that the school takes responsibility for assessing the completed work and in ensuring the child's access to the full curriculum

- pupils have a consistent network of visiting teachers as they travel, to monitor and support them with their work

- parents take responsibility for the practical support of their children and that they collaborate closely with the schools and TESS

- a national policy is put in place promoting school based distance learning. This is essential if distance learning is not to become a second rate and separate provision.

Some families travel seasonally but without the key elements for operating distance learning work, for example, without a base school or a planned touring season. Some Gypsy children travel seasonally for fieldwork or harvesting, travelling abroad for parents' work purposes. Distance learning work can be a useful continuity strategy if sufficient contact can be organised through visiting teachers from TESS. Sometimes, in the absence of visiting teachers or use of the new technologies, children travelling abroad for periods can only be supplied with work packs to keep them in touch with learning in an attempt to maintain motivation and prevent regression. It is not always possible in these situations for the cycle of distance learning to operate actively and the workpack is a weaker but necessary alternative.

It is the workpack rather than distance learning work which may be provided by TESS for highly mobile young people without a legal place to stay and whose families are subject to frequent eviction. As the children have no regular legal home or base school on which to base distance learning, workpacks offer alternative, albeit limited, support.

4

Legislation, policies and initiatives that affect Gypsies and Travellers

In education children cannot be seen in isolation from their families, and education cannot be seen in isolation from health, welfare and accommodation needs for families who experience difficulty in trying to access basic services. However the very existence of Traveller families in some local authorities is a contradictory one for different authority personnel. For example,

> The bizarre situation may exist where, within a local authority, a department exists with a budget specifically geared to preventing Gypsies and other Travellers camping in the area, evicting them if they do manage it and then organising the land in a way afterwards that prevents their return – ditching, banking, fencing etc. At the same time within that same area health or education authority, there may also be special initiatives to support families' access to services ...(WMCESTC, 1995).

Education
Parental Duty
In educational legislation parents have responsibilities. Section 7 of the Education Act (1996) imposes the duty on parents to secure the education of their children

> It shall be the duty of the parent of every child of compulsory school age to cause him to receive efficient full-time education suitable to his age,

ability and aptitude and to any special educational needs he may have either by regular attendance at school or otherwise.

Local Education Authority Duty

LEAs are expected to ensure sufficient places for the area to afford all pupils opportunities for education relative to their ages, abilities, aptitudes and any special educational needs they may have (section 411 of the Education Act 1996). Also LEAs have a duty to make arrangements enabling all parents in their area to express a preference as to which school they wish their child to attend. The LEA duty extends to *all* children residing in their area, whether permanently or temporarily, so that 'the duty thus embraces in particular Traveller children, including Gypsies' (DES Circular 1/81, Paragraph 5).

School Attendance Order

The LEA is expected to take action when a child of compulsory school age is found not to be registered in any school (Section 437 of the Education Act 1996).

The LEA has a duty to monitor attendance

The LEA has responsibility to institute proceedings in relation to non-school attendance offences (section 446 of the Education Act 1996).

Responsibility of Schools

Schools must report unauthorised absences of two weeks or more and other irregular attendances to the LEA. Schools are encouraged to have policies and strategies in place to effect good attendance. Where they have not been notified of the reason for a child's absence, schools are encouraged to make first day follow up to find out why a child is absent.

Travelling Families – Dual Registration

To protect the continuity of learning of Traveller children, the Pupil Registration Regulation (with effect from January 1998), facilitates dual registration of Traveller children in schools as they travel. Families who travel regularly or seasonally but always return to a fixed home base and the local base school can benefit from dual registration.

If the parents or TESS inform the base school that the child is going be away travelling but will return, or if the school knows that the child comes from a Traveller family which regularly or seasonally travels away from the area, then regulation 9 (1) (b) (registration at another school) and (g) (absence in excess of four weeks, unknown location) no longer requires the pupil to be removed from the base school register.

While the Traveller child is away, the base school holds the place open and records the absence as Authorised (register code T).

Children can register in schools as they travel without fear of losing their place in their base school.

School Attendance, Policy and Practice on Categorisation of Absence, DfEE 1994 states:

> Some schools (where children travel away from the school) are able to maintain contact with the children by outreach work or distance learning packs, although such activities should not be viewed as a preferable alternative to attendance at school ... all effort should be made to encourage maintenance of attendance at school.

Section 444 Protection from Prosecution (Education Act 1996)

Under subsection 1, if a child of compulsory school age who is a registered pupil at a school fails to attend regularly at the school, the parent of the child is guilty of an offence. The circumstances are identified in which the parent of a child shall be acquitted if they can prove:

a) that he is engaged in a trade or business of such a nature as to require him to travel from place to place

b) that the child has attended a school as a registered pupil as regularly as the nature of that trade or business permits, and

c) if the child has attained the age of six years, that he/she has made at least two hundred attendances (*100 days*) during the period of twelve months ending with the date on which proceedings were instituted.

The spirit of the legislation is to protect families from unreasonable prosecution when travelling for work purposes and this makes full time schooling impossible. It is not intended to reduce Traveller children's equal entitlement to full time education, nor to imply that part time education is sufficient. Parents still have a duty to make sure their children are receiving education suitable to their needs when not in school.

Where children are provided with distance learning work whilst travelling, there is a duty on parents to supervise them in carrying out their work. Government regulations urge school attendance in line with the majority population yet requests sensitivity and sympathy when considering individual Traveller families. The DfES view is that:

> I think it is necessary to adopt a pragmatic approach. The aim should always be to ensure that such children attend school as regularly as possible and regard school as something to be looked forward to rather than seeing it as an alien experience. A difficult balance must be struck between, on the one hand, the need for action in individual cases in the interests of the child and, on the other, adopting a sensitive and sympathetic approach which recognises the particular circumstances and lifestyle of the family concerned (DfES, 2003).

Admissions

Admissions procedures in schools and LEAs have particular significance for Traveller children seeking to enter a school outside the normal admissions period. In an attempt to reduce the practice of local children moving between schools mid term because of dispute, disaffection and exclusion, some LEAs, in partnership with schools, have prescribed regulations for admissions. These may include Admissions Boards or Forums sitting regularly to allocate places.

These local regulations should not discriminate against Gypsy and Traveller children coming into an area and accessing school places.

Admission Forums are required to consider the allocation of places to other children who arrive outside the normal admission round when popular schools are full, so that all schools play their part in accommodating these children and not just those unpopular with parents and which have spare places (Schools Admissions Code of Practice January 2003).

It is the role of Admissions Forums in LEAs to secure fair school admissions policies and the duty of the LEA to provide places for all children including Gypsy and Traveller children whether in the area permanently or temporarily.

Infant class size: treatment of Traveller children

As part of the Government's drive to raise standards in schools in 1998, they focused on children in the early years at school where their learning would underpin the rest of their education, and highlighted the provision of smaller class sizes as a big advantage in the process. Legislation has been passed to ensure that from September 2001, with some exceptions, no 5, 6 or 7 year old would be in a class of more than thirty pupils. Additional money was identified (£620 million) to enable LEAs and schools to comply with the limit.

All LEAs are required to submit plans setting out how the limit is to be achieved for their area. The DfES provided guidance to LEAs on how to prepare the statements: The guidance refers to 'exceptions' and permits:

> an exception to the limit where a pupil moves into the area outside the normal admissions round and there is no other school which would provide suitable education within reasonable distance of his home. In this case, such a pupil can be treated as an exception to the class size limit for the remainder of that academic year. Traveller children are most likely to fall within this category (para 10b).

The guidance points out that many LEAs will have details of regular and predictable movements of Travellers and these pupils will often count as excepted. It suggests that these movements be taken into account in the LEA's planning and that they set out the proposed arrangements for dealing with such pupils in their plans.

The DfES wants as far as possible to ensure that Traveller children are not refused admission in circumstances where they could be regarded as excepted pupils.

Government measures to assist LEAs and schools in meeting the needs of Gypsy and Traveller children

Funding support to LEAs to provide Traveller services has been available nationally since the 1980s through a national pool funding arrangement and through a competitive bidding system. The aim has been for services to: 'create unhindered access to and full integration in mainstream education for Gypsy and Traveller children' (DES, 1990). The funding supports provision for Traveller children designed to:

- improve access to schools
- improve regular school attendance
- support higher levels of attainment

The grant funds the provision of Traveller Education Support Services to support LEAs, schools and Traveller families. They generally consist of:

- adviser and co-ordinators
- peripatetic advisory and support teachers
- education welfare or field welfare staff
- classroom assistants
- transport and uniform budget
- teaching and learning resources including culture specific material
- pupil education record transfer
- professional development and inset provision

Until recently, funding was provided through the Standards Fund Traveller Achievement Grant (TAG), which consisted of a proportion from both the DfES (52%), and the LEA (48%).

Consultation has taken place on moving from a competitive bidding system to a needs based formula. Initial models proved bureaucratically unwieldy and a simpler numbers based exercise was rushed through to replace existing arrangements. Because this exercise generally lacked a clear information structure and was inconsistently applied there was a need for further discussion and negotiation.

However, it was announced in December 2002 that TAG was to be deleted in April 2003 and funding for the education support services for Gypsy and Traveller children would be merged into a new Standards Fund Grant, the Vulnerable Children's Grant.

The grant represents the interests of a whole range of children in the LEA such as Gypsies and Travellers, refugees and asylum seekers, pregnant school girls, excluded pupils, looked after children, as well as the reintegration of young offenders. Although the total grant is ring fenced, money within it is not, and therefore is vulnerable to virement across the grant and between a range of needy groups.

Experience at a national and European level shows Traveller education has made most progress where funding has been focused specifically on the target groups and not subjected to competing against other interests. There has been limited planning opportunity for reorganisation of expenditure in the first year of the grant, but the competition across the grant from different LEA interests is significant and raises concern for Traveller provision in future.

The DfES consultation document *Aiming High* (2003) is aimed at the future of the Ethnic Minority Achievement Grant. DfES held three conferences across the country to launch the consultation. The inclusion of Travellers in the document is at best unclear but can be seen as relevant with regard to two questions posed by the document on mobility.

- what specific action should the Department take to minimise high levels of mobility?

- what specific action should the Department take to manage high levels of mobility?

Responses with regard to minimising the high mobility of the Gypsy and Traveller population have no doubt focused on the difference between *planned* mobility and *enforced* mobility, notably through the regular eviction of families travelling for work purposes with no legal place to resort to short term. The much used phrase 'joined up government' links this question directly to the accommodation needs of Gypsies and Travellers and the impact of under provision and failure to plan, on educational stability and planning.

Adequate and regularly reviewed provision of a range of required site accommodation, local schools and health services would be helpful to those developing expertise and curriculum to meet the needs of Gypsy and Traveller children and families wanting to settle on sites locally, or moving in a planned process between legal accommodation stops. Planned mobility can be organised but it is enforced and erratic mobility which disables and undermines family confidence and the ability of service providers to deliver well.

How influential joined up government can be remains to be seen, but there are existing duties and requirements in place which if rigorously applied could deliver a decent accommodation plan to meet the needs of the relatively small communities of Gypsies and Travellers without a legal place to stay. The kinds of response the DfES would need to take to manage high levels of mobility in relation to Gypsies and Travellers, would vary, but would certainly include a range of tried and tested education continuity strategies and a call for a national strategy for school based distance learning. Innovation in relation to the use of new technologies to manage mobility has to be high on the agenda, while allocating additional funding to schools regularly experiencing significant turnover of pupils is just common sense.

Ethnic Monitoring, Race Relations (Amendment) Act 2000 and Racist Incident Forms

In January 2003, Gypsy, Roma and Travellers of Irish Heritage were included in the DfES ethnic categories list which LEAs and schools sent to all parents inviting them to ascribe an ethnicity for their children (children over the age of 11 could independently ascribe). The consultation exercise aimed to provide the information for schools to enable them to monitor the achievements of all children in terms of ethnicity and, in particular, to analyse and respond to those ethnic groups consistently underachieving. There is also a reporting duty on schools to the LEA so that underachievement information can inform planning and external support. The data is also reported nationally.

Under the Race Relations (Amendment) Act 2000, schools are obliged to have in place a race equality policy and action plan in line with the duty to promote good race relations. Schools are also required to complete and return an LEA reporting form on racist incidents in the school so that LEAs can monitor the level of racist incidents in schools and identify where schools may need support in addressing the problem. Teachers may need opportunities for training in order to use the Racist Incident Report Form confidently.

The formal identification of Gypsies and Travellers has not pre-viously been given any priority at national level for education monitoring purposes. The general national census categories do not include these groups. There is significant evidence to show that many parents have had difficulty in responding to the DfES ethnic category exercise for fear of negative repercussions as a result of their self identification. Many families have spent years trying to keep their heads down to avoid identification and the expected con-sequences. This indicates that much work needs to be done to inform and create parental awareness of the purpose of the exercise, the benefits it can bring to their children and the responsibilities of the schools to address children's needs.

School administrative staff, who are usually the first contact when parents register their child, need to be well trained in welcoming and supporting parents, especially when describing the purpose and benefit of ethnic categorisation for educational purposes.

DfES, LEAs and schools have much to do before parents have sufficient confidence in their intentions in order to feel safe enough to declare their ethnicity.

Government funding measures to address local disadvantage

There are three major funding streams created by government to address disadvantage in school age children: Sure Start (3-5 years), Children's Fund (5-13 years) and Connexions (14-19 years). Travellers are one of the target groups included in the national measures for local actions to address disadvantage and under-achievement. There are growing examples around the country where the needs of Gypsy and Traveller children have been included in planning and development:

Sure Start

This programme has supported:

- playgrounds on or adjacent to sites
- culture specific early learning materials, picture books etc
- provision of Early Years Integration Workers for mobile Travellers

- cultural awareness training for staff

Unfortunately some geographically based projects have felt unable to include or are reticent about including children of mobile families in their activities. Their operational inflexibilities continue to exclude the most marginalised children. However, the best examples demonstrate the potential of initiatives to include and make a difference to Gypsy and Traveller children's lives.

Children's Fund

This fund has supported providers in establishing projects including:

- homework support workers
- out of school play and youth link worker for Travellers
- consultants to befriend and record Traveller children's views on education and needs to represent to LEA officers and Children's Fund nationally
- cultural awareness training for staff

Connexions

Aimed at the older age group, this fund offers:

- provision of specialist adviser for Travellers
- active inclusion of Gypsy and Traveller youngsters in an adviser's workload
- identification of more culturally relevant and motivating work experience opportunities
- cultural awareness training for Connexions staff

Health

There is persistent evidence about the poor health of Traveller communities. They have less access to GPs, health centres and clinics and are difficult to track and locate by health professionals when travelling and on temporary sites, with the result that:

> the health of the Gypsy and Traveller communities is amongst the poorest among ethnic minority groups with a higher incidence of stillbirth and neonatal death and a higher incidence of accident from the appalling conditions in which some families are forced to live...

> Gypsies and Travellers continue to experience difficulties in gaining and maintaining access to primary healthcare services and obtaining referral to secondary healthcare (Morris and Clements, 1999).

Also, 'twice as many low birth weight babies are born to Traveller mothers (12.8%) than the national average (6.9%)' (Pahl and Vaile, 1986).

While all communities have a right in law to access free health care at the point of need, many Gypsies and Travellers continue to have difficulty obtaining health care. Families without a permanent address still find themselves refused treatment by some GPs and clinics despite legislation covering temporary registration. Advocates who follow up on their behalf are usually referred to another willing GP for treatment. Yet no steps are taken to ensure the refusing GP undertakes the responsibility.

Left to themselves, many families who are refused treatment by GPs resort to inappropriate use of Accident and Emergency services at hospitals. Some Health Trusts provide dedicated health visitor time for Travellers to catch up on health support as a result of historical neglect and in recognition of ongoing access difficulties. This includes support to access local services and provides training for colleagues on the health needs of Travellers to prepare them and raise expectations for their involvement in the future.

Families often view school medicals and nurses as being different from and less important than other general medical services. Traveller families need to be familiar with all medical and health services and this will often require additional communication. The need for patient held health records, particularly for mobile Travellers, would assist continuity of health care. This system has been piloted locally in some parts of the country but is not yet nationwide.

Although Travellers have the lowest life expectancy rate and the highest infant mortality rate in the UK, Health Service Circular 1998/229 states that: 'assessing the health needs of people from minority ethnic groups does not include the needs/access problems of Gypsies and Travellers' (Royal College of Physicians, 1988).

Nevertheless in some areas the healthcare needs of Travellers are written into the Public Health Reports and Planning documents and some Primary Care Trusts have identified roles and responsibilities for staff to work with Travellers, homeless and minority ethnic communities.

Accommodation: recent history

The 1968 Caravan Sites Act is often hailed by some as the only Act having been of any benefit to Travellers. The Act placed a duty on LAs to make site provision for Travellers residing in or resorting to their area. For the purpose of the Act a Gypsy was defined as a person of nomadic habit of life whatever their race or origin.

To further encourage site building the LAs which did build sites could apply for 'designation' status which amounted to a quota system of Traveller families allowed in the area with increased powers for the LAs to evict those families over and above the quota. Despite 100 per cent grants for the building of new sites, councils were slow to provide them.

In 1994 the Criminal Justice and Public Order Act (CJPOA) repealed the 1968 Caravan Sites Act, its duty to provide sites and the capital grants to fund building of sites, and the Secretary of State's power to direct LAs to provide sites. Although over 30 per cent of the community had no legal place to stay and many LAs had not complied with the 1968 Caravan Sites Act, the government of the day took the view that enough public provision of sites had been made and Gypsies and Travellers should be encouraged to provide their own sites.

In addition, the CJPOA accorded strong new powers to LAs and the police to evict families. The civil trespass status became criminal trespass punishable in law if families did not comply with a direction to leave 'as soon as practicable', or re-entered the land within three months of the direction order. Unofficial encampments of more than six vehicles could now be evicted. The only defence not to comply is as a result of mechanical breakdown, illness or other immediate emergency.

There are detailed conditions under which LAs may tolerate short-term unauthorised camping where families are not 'causing a level of nuisance' (Circular 18/94 *Gypsy Sites Policy and Unauthorised Camping*, 2000). LAs can also examine ways of minimising the level of nuisance on tolerated sites by providing basic services for families such as toilets, a refuse skip and a supply of drinking water. The emphasis is on the need for all concerned to negotiate a mutually acceptable date for leaving the site.

Statutory Duties

The above circular also details LAs' obligations under other legislation. Social service departments and local housing authorities are reminded of their obligations under Part 111 of the Children Act 1989 (Local Authority Support for Children and Families) and Part 111 of the Housing Act 1985 (Housing the Homeless) that:

> The Secretaries of State expect authorities to take careful account of these obligations when taking decisions about the future maintenance of authorised Gypsy caravan sites and the eviction of persons from unauthorised sites.

LEAs are required to bear in mind that their statutory duties 'should take careful account of the effects of an eviction on the education of children already enrolled or in the process of being enrolled at a school. Where an authority decides to proceed with an eviction and any families concerned move elsewhere in the same area, alternative educational arrangements must be made in accordance with the requirements of the law appropriate to the children's ages, abilities and aptitudes'. Local Authorities who intend to evict are also expected to liaise with other local authorities which may have statutory duties to fulfil in respect of those persons being evicted.

LAs are also reminded that families may be receiving assistance from local health or welfare services and that they should liaise with the relevant statutory agencies to ensure that they are not prevented from fulfilling their obligations towards Traveller families.

Planning

The Government when introducing the CJPOA stated that in repealing the 1968 Caravan Sites Act, local authorities should encourage Travellers to provide for themselves.

Research carried out on behalf of the Department of the Environment, Transport and the Regions by the Advisory Committee for the Education of Romany and other Travellers (ACERT) showed that nearly two thirds of authorities did not have a Gypsy policy in their Local Plans. The DETR sent a letter to all Chief Planning Officers in May 1998 drawing attention to the research outcomes and providing guidance to planning authorities in making progress (Morris and Clements, 1999). This guidance included reminding LAs of their statutory duties to Travellers under the key pieces of legislation including homelessness, and also the need to consult Travellers and their representatives regarding accommodation needs at the early stages of preparing structure, local and unitary plans.

In *Broadening Horizons* a reference is made to the House of Commons Report (vol 241 cols 315-320) about the fact that over 90 per cent of planning applications by Travellers are refused permission to proceed (Naylor and Wild-Smith, 1997).

Europe

In May 1989, two significant resolutions were passed in respect of the education of Gypsies and Travellers and Occupational Travellers such as Showmen, Circus, and Bargees.

* Resolution of the Council and the Ministries of Education meeting with the Council 22 May 1989 on school provision for the children of *Occupational Travellers* (89/c/53/01, Luxembourg)

* Resolution of the Council and the Ministries of Education meeting with the Council 22 May 1989 on school provision for *Gypsy and Traveller children* (89/c/53/02, Luxembourg)

The resolutions in brief called on Member States to take action to improve the education for the children of the named communities and to promote education provision. At the end of 1993 Member States were required to report on progress being made and the *Report on the Implementation of Measures Envisaged in the Resolutions* demonstrated that although there had been some progress there was still much to be done:

> Bit by bit families are taking on more books and schooling is on the rise. The children will read – and then they will write, enriching European culture with their contributions. These children must have the oppor-

tunity to get into school, to stay in school and to be personally and culturally respected while there (EC, 1966).

When introducing its funded education projects programme SOCRATES in 1995 the Commission specifically targeted Gypsy and Traveller children. In the second phase of the programme cycle, SOCRATES 11, Gypsies and Travellers were not specifically targeted although projects aimed at them could be included under broader headlines around social inclusion and intercultural education.

The Commission are currently consulting on the target groups and programmes needed for the third phase (2006). Strong representation has been made by a number of UK education, parent and professional organisations to ensure that Gypsies, Travellers and Occupational Travellers are specifically targeted, particularly in light of pending enlargement where the new Member States from eastern Europe have a significant population of Roma with little experience of formal education.

The United Nations Convention on the Rights of the Child

The United Kingdom is a signatory to the UN Rights of the Child. The 54 articles include Article 30, gives rights to children in a community with other members of their group, to enjoy their culture, practise their religion and use their own language.

In 1995 the United Nations Committee published a report on how the signatory states were making progress in providing for children. They recommended that the United Kingdom take proactive measures for the rights of Gypsy and Traveller children including their right to education and the provision of sufficient well-serviced caravan sites to live on.

In 1995, the United Nations recognised Roma as an official minority.

The Human Rights Act (Oct 2000)

The Human Rights Act is a significant piece of constitutional legislation through which a Government can encourage a modern civic society where the rights and responsibilities of citizens are recognised and balanced. It means that in order to claim rights, people no longer need to go to the European Court in Strasbourg because they can claim them under the European Convention on Human Rights in UK Courts. The Act requires all public authorities in the UK to bring policy and practice into line with Convention rights.

The Act may have particular importance for Gypsy and Traveller families. Civil rights lawyers have already taken cases to the Human Rights Court in Strasbourg with regard to the alleged failure of the UK courts to act appropriately in planning application procedures particularly where families are seeking to live on land they own (Article 8.1).

The Human Rights Act is now being used in British courts by legal representatives to defend planning applications and appeals on behalf of Gypsy and Traveller families. At further risk could be local authorities and police in areas where families are being constantly evicted and where there is no authorised site provision and no toleration allowed. As a consequence, many of the policies need testing in practice to ensure that they are appropriate, non-discriminatory and reflective of democratic actions in a democratic society.

5

Traveller education: case stories and action research

Practitioner research or action research (AR) is a means of gathering information to change or improve educational practice in schools, other educational institutions or organisations. Through practitioner research teachers and advisors and other educational professionals learn to develop skills which enhance their understanding of the contexts within which they work. Case stories are included in this book. They demonstrate the freedom and limits of professional agency to intervene, change and ameliorate practices that are perceived to hinder the inclusion and educational development of Traveller pupils in schools. The case stories enable their authors, readers and participants to develop a deeper understanding of the ambiguities, inconsistencies and constraints they faced in everyday practice.

To identify the challenges to teachers and other educational professionals engaged in the schooling and development of Traveller children, practitioner or action research has been adopted as an explicit means of change. Changing attitudes, values and understanding through investigation and research is a powerful way to counteract prejudice or racism towards Travellers and to promote a more meaningful and effective education for Traveller children. The process is predominantly a professional one, used to ameliorate or eradicate inequitable or unjust practices in educational contexts. In the professional development of Traveller education professional action research changes personal perspectives at the same time as influencing other research participants.

The case stories included in this book are insider accounts written by teachers and advisory support teachers about their investigations into Traveller education and their attempts to clarify the current situation and take steps to change or improve it. The main priority for their research is always the participation and inclusion of Traveller children in educational practices in mainstream schooling. Each case story comes from a different area of the UK. Most describe issues of racism and discrimination in the education of Traveller children and the attempts to counteract them. They illustrate how professionals, who are given the brief of supporting the education of Traveller children, struggle with bureaucracy, negative attitudes, and physical and emotional barriers created by their clients' marginalisation.

Action research allows the professionals concerned to use their professional roles for insider access to the contexts described. It gives them flexibility because they can be responsive to the moraes of the situation and interpret it through a process involving reflexivity and self-evaluation. The fundamental aims of action research are to improve practice as well as to produce new knowledge. The new knowledge produced and utilised by the research is used to make decisions about what is possible and expedient to change in the light of the evidence collected.

The development of practitioner discrimination and judgement increases with the complexity of social situations. The process of investigation combined with making decisions about what is best for Traveller children benefits from the involvement of like-minded colleagues. The support of a group of sympathetic professionals who are willing to discuss evidence, its significance and implications is crucial. It ensures that decisions about what needs to be done are balanced and equitable because of a wider ratification and interpretation of the evidence presented.

The main characteristic of action research is that it is a process of investigation which examines a practical situation experienced by educational professionals that is problematic, unpredictable and demanding. It adopts an exploratory stance aimed at deepening understanding of a situation. It interprets the situation from the viewpoint of the participants, who are the main investigators and others contributing to the research, including children. It aims to describe and explain the situation in plain language and in doing so it tells a story about the concerns of the investigation within the context in which it is set. There are four fundamental aspects of the process of action research: reflection on the research concerns; investigation of the situation; planning changes and monitoring them; actively realising the plans with interpretation and reflection on the evidence gathered.

To begin the process the teacher or professional selects a research question or issue related to investigating Traveller education as inclusive practice. It may be a question, an issue or concern about Traveller pupils making progress in literacy in a particular class or school. The decision to focus on pupils' literacy progress necessitates initial investigation of the question or issue identified, and collecting evidence to confirm that the topic is a genuine one and worth investigation. The initial investigation and observation will then support or invalidate the research topic as originally conceived. At this stage the focus may be redefined or reframed to fit a new perspective or understanding. After which the investigation then proceeds to gather evidence, and monitor and plan action aimed to improve the practical situation. The basic process consists of reflection, investigation, planning and action.

The first step in action research for any educational purpose is *reflection* on an issue or research question which defines, in general terms, the focus of the subsequent investigation. The initial question is usually a potent issue, and has a strong value laden association or heart-felt personal ownership. The beginning of the process is thinking about what needs to be changed, and why the issue is felt, or seen to be in need of change. Defining the research issue means to articulate it, share it with colleagues, explain it in some sense and then find a means to investigate it. Reflection at the start of the research ensures that a focus is chosen which is genuine, worthwhile and makes a contribution to improved educational Traveller practice. Reflection is integral to the total investigatory process in AR.

Reflection involves reconstructing and reframing activities through evidence recorded in the investigation, monitoring and observing planned action. It can take place when investigating or later when opportunities arise for reviewing the evidence. It can be a solitary or a group activity: a solitary activity if writing in a journal or diary, or a group activity when discussing the evidence with friends or colleagues informally or in a professional group. Reflection involves reinterpretating the evidence to uncover hidden assumptions and challenges which can be seen in unexpected or unpredicted outcomes. It aims to evaluate whether evidence confirms the planned direction for further action, or indicates a need for change and redirection. However, opportunities for professionals to transform resides in their potential to reflect-on-action (O'Hanlon, 1993), that is when they are actually interpreting evidence of their practices in light of the evidence collected.

Reflection may take place on three recognised levels (Aristotle, 1977; Habermas, 1986; Grundy, 1982):

• on the technical level, where the professional considers the best way to reach an accepted but unexamined goal, e.g. set curriculum targets

• on the practical level, where the professional examines the means of achieving the goals as well as the goal itself and its implications, by asking questions about what should be happening in the best interests of Traveller children and young people, for example, reflection on and observation of educational strategies and methods to gain the best learning in educational situations

• and on the critical level, where moral and ethical issues concerned with social justice, equality, power and control are considered along with the methods and the intentions of the research plan. It is intrinsically political – for example, transforming schools, educational attitudes and community acceptance of fully inclusive practices.

In the process of reflection each professional reviews, reconstructs and critically interprets their own practices through grounding their explanations in their evidence. The aim in action research is to produce professionals who are able to apply educational principles and techniques within a framework of their own experience, contextual factors, and social and philosophical values. Competent reflective practitioners address why specific Traveller educational practice exists before examining how best to deliver it. They make decisions about change on a sound practical basis validated in the enquiry process. Reflection on practice leads to a willingness to examine and re-examine the possibilities for the schooling and education of Traveller children from a variety of perspectives and theoretical viewpoints. It challenges accepted educational orthodoxies because they are often unexamined and repeated indiscriminately in differentiated and complex contexts. The action research process requires professionals to apply their skills in contextually appropriate ways, which requires different responses in specific situations in schools and the wider community where Traveller education is practiced.

Investigation is initially the confirmation of a research question or issue in the practical situation and begins with initial collection of evidence to endorse, or otherwise, the original idea. Investigation, or observation, may confirm the need to continue to examine the teaching of literacy more deeply, or it may indicate a need to redirect the focus a little. For example, the question of investigating literacy strategies for Traveller pupils may become one of general re-organisation and differentiation of literacy strategies for all pupils.

The teacher may ask how literacy progress is measured, why progress is generally considered to be fast or slow, what teaching strategies are currently being employed and why, and whether the particular Traveller's background and age, and length of time out of school demands special consideration and if so how? If the evidence collected confirms that the research question deserves deeper investigation, then the researcher can continue to interpret the evidence from the initial observations and redefine the question or issue more specifically in light of the new data. If however, the initial data collection doesn't support the need to continue the investigation, then the teacher has the opportunity to reframe the research question or refocus the enquiry for example, an investigation of literacy teaching strategies generally, to ensure the inclusion of all pupils in a classroom or school.

Planning and making changes is a form of constructed action, and by definition it must be forward looking and based on the evidence already collected. It must be flexible in relation to unforeseen circumstances and constraints. It should be chosen to allow the professional to act in a more educationally effective way, over a greater range of circumstances, and with more understanding of what works for Traveller pupils. Estimating the outcomes of the action provides the rationale for the intended changes. As part of the planning, before taking action, discussing possible courses of action with others, particularly colleagues and participants, is essential, as too is reflecting on the earlier evidence. That other people share the evidence and discuss its implications for action is crucial for balanced planning. If there is a group of like-minded professionals investigating Traveller education issues, the main researcher can use their feedback before planning any deliberate action. Checking with someone else before action is taken can avoid unwise or hasty decisions. Any feedback from a friend, colleague or wider group must be based on mutual trust, confidence and understanding.

Action refers to the implementation of deliberate and controlled changes to educational practice. After constructive discussion and reflection, professionals put their ideas into action in the real situation, and monitor their effects in order to judge success. Action must be planned and intentional because of the nature of the changing circumstances in dynamic educational situations. Exercising practical judgement in the implementation of the plan may require skilful negotiation and an element of risk-taking in the situation. Actions and their consequences should be recorded and evaluated. Judgements about their success and effectiveness can then be evaluated by participants, or arbitrated by friends or colleagues. The evaluation is best when it comes from someone familiar with the investigation and who can be trusted to give balanced and constructive feedback.

A research diary or journal is a useful means of reflection. It enables the main researcher and participants to keep a record of the investigative journey and its effects on professionalism, self-understanding and educational development. Reflective practice is an important resource for professional reconstruction and taking stock, where professionals view themselves primarily as agents of change, identifying and reconstructing the significant aspects of their relevant experiences that are specific to the improvement of Traveller education. The experiences recorded may be predominantly professional but occasionally more personal experiences may impinge, and writing a journal may become a more personally reflective and emotionally satisfying exercise.

Reflection, observation, planning and action are often referred to within a spiral of research. Although these are the key activities of AR, it is fundamentally organised and planned practitioner inquiry about professionals' practices, regardless of the many technical definitions. Many terms such as spiral, insider, outsider, collaborative, critical, technical, practical, diagnostic, participant, empirical, experimental and emancipatory have been used when defining AR (Zeichner, 1993). However, most distinctive definitions of AR emphasise the importance of the process itself as leading to change through new knowledge and understanding.

There is considerable debate about the extent to which AR is a research methodology or technique, or a broad approach to social research and reform. Action research is concerned with the development of teachers' and other professionals' theories of education and their practical social agency. It raises questions about social and educational change, improvement, reform and innovation. In professional development which uses AR, every practitioner implicitly evolves a social, political and moral practical dimension which is embedded in their work. Every routine professional action reveals ethical commitments to social continuity and change whether we admit it or not. We cannot be entirely neutral when making deliberate changes in social and educational contexts (O'Hanlon, 1993). Also, practitioner research allows space for reflection on the bias of the participants. Personal reflection via journals and notebooks is encouraged as part of the process of self-understanding. Knowing our values and attitudes which reveal themselves in the research evidence of our practice enables deeper understanding of why specific judgements and decisions are being made. Decisions made throughout the investigatory process can support new insights and change existing situations and behaviour. The understandings may direct the professional's actions and practice in a new way.

The critique and debate raised by professionals and participants in AR has made people more aware of the need to see and hear the meaning of cultural difference and its significance. Professional development involving forms of investigation that are collaborative, inclusive, supportive and supported, focused on developing more equal and just educational practice, can be achieved through AR. It is particularly successful with the additional help of colleagues or a group of like-minded people to support and discuss evidence and its interpretation (see O'Hanlon, 2003).

Discussion on procedures and methods can be lengthy but our intention is to illustrate the grounding of the AR approach to data interpretation in a specific perspective like the case stories in this book. The ideal of social justice and equity in Traveller education is intrinsically, if not explicitly, embedded in the stories outlined in the next section. We leave the reader to identify the neutrality or otherwise of the case stories presented.

The case stories are built upon current accepted educational principles that:

• most Traveller children attend their local schools as far as possible, and stay in the main classroom with appropriate support for most of the school day or week

• all teachers in a school take responsibility for Traveller learning, with appropriate resources and opportunities for whole school staff and professional development

• teachers understand the constraints of intermittent schooling, seasonal absence and high mobility

• schools rethink their inclusive values, how they affect their organisational practice through curriculum and assessment arrangements; monitoring the full participation of Traveller pupils; using a range of teaching strategies to suit diverse learning needs; meeting pupils' social, emotional and pastoral needs; supporting parent partnership; and evaluating everyday practice

• Traveller support services do what they can to ensure that Traveller children have access to whatever educational opportunities are afforded the general population.

These aims are implicit in the case stories. Collaboration and team-work supported by democratic discursive procedures have been used to create the case stories. This process lessens the pressure on lone individuals in professional roles to meet diverse problems related to Traveller education.

Action Research case stories

Although the case stories which follow began along AR lines they have been abbreviated, edited and re-written as stories about educational intervention for Traveller children. AR can work simul-taneously at different levels from the classroom to the LEA and nationally. It can influence the continuum from professional practice to policy making. Teachers and other professionals need to use what-ever means of change will impact on the educational culture, its values, attitudes and practices in the long-term. Traveller teachers and advisers who carried out the investigations have developed skills to enhance their understanding of educational complexity through a deeper understanding of practical decisions made to foster the full inclusion of Traveller pupils in schools.

Our educational system seeks to be inclusive regardless of pupils' ethnicity or way of life. When the National Curriculum was esta-blished in 1988, the Secretary of State for Education requested that guidance be issued to ensure that the curriculum take account of the ethnic and cultural diversity of British society and the importance of the curriculum in promoting equal opportunity for all pupils, regard-less of their gender or ethnic origin.

Action or practitioner research for inclusive practice challenge the school system's support for marginalised groups like Travellers and children with additional or special education needs. Case story accounts of attempts to make schools and LA policy and practice more inclusive for all pupils aim to demonstrate what is possible by committed professionals within a short time. The case stories may begin as an investigation on a small scale but they can grow in their reach and influence on many levels in society. It is difficult to know exactly how or when deliberate educational interventions on behalf of Traveller children influence and ameliorate unjust situations now or in the future. What is recounted in this book are observed and immediate changes in the situations described. Any changes brought about to the attitudes, actions or values of others are less amenable to recording for our purposes.

The AR accounts are chosen because of their unique professional function within a particular community, where they allow the participants and their readers to access people and situations not normally reached by outside researchers. They are predominately a form of qualitative research focused on insider situations. Each professional, because of their role, has privileged access to Travellers and as such they can be described as insiders. They all acknowledge their subjective stance, and claim that their accounts are valid and authentic because they have reflected about their interests, bias and commitment to Traveller education. Recognising their own personal value perspective is fundamental to the reflective process. The cases have been individually and ethically reported through the acknowledgement of realism and its control in the research process. This is achieved by firstly endorsing and recognising the varied and diverse values and attitudes of research participants (including the main researcher). These values and attitudes are inherent in the evidence gathered and are therefore open to scrutiny and challenge. Secondly, the research participants, through their interpretation of different research evidence, may revise their understandings and thus create new knowledge.

The case stories have used interviews, discussions, photography, field notes, journals, questionnaires, triangulation and observation, with the aid of video and audio recorders. They have applied the four themes of reflection, investigation, planning and action as recurring and integrated aspects of the research process. Although the specific focus is on action as an outcome of the research, this is not always planned action. Action can be construed as a form of agency during investigative intervention. Let the stories speak for themselves.

6

Case Stories

1. Do schools reflect Traveller culture?

Jill works in a new unitary authority, which includes some small villages, as well a large urban area established as a new town some thirty years ago. The town is still in a state of development, but it has several long established schools as well as some new ones. She is co-ordinator of the Local Education Authority Traveller Education Support Service (TESS). There are two established local authority sites for Travellers in the town, which have been in existence longer than some parts of the town. The children of the families living on these sites attend local school. There is also a continually changing population of families in the area, who have no legal place to stay. Most of the families are from either the Gypsy Traveller or Irish Traveller community. From time to time some Traveller families move in and out of housing in the area for varying periods. Some families have lived in the area so long that their grandchildren are now of school age.

During a local school Ofsted inspection, Jill was asked what the school did to reflect Traveller culture. Later, on reflection, she realised she hadn't answered the question adequately and that it needed further investigation. Were the schools doing what she had said they were, or were they doing something quite different? Were schools in the area reflecting Traveller culture and if not why not? A plan of action for the TESS to promote multicultural education required further investigation.

How could Jill observe the situation in order to formulate an answer to the question raised? It would be difficult because of time constraints to look at all the schools in the LEA, so a sample of schools was chosen for the case study or story. Eight primary schools were chosen: First, Middle and Combined schools ranging from year 1 to year 7 with children from 4 to 11 years old. Children of families living on one of the LA sites, attended two First and two Middle schools nearby. These schools had Traveller children on roll over a long period. Recently Traveller children had started attending a Middle school, and one of the First schools in the area regularly had Traveller children during the summer term when families camped nearby. These schools seemed like obvious choices for the study and two additional schools, a First and Combined school, that had never had Traveller children were also included to provide a balance. One of the Middle schools had a very large intake of children not from its local catchment area. The schools had a varied intake and were located in different parts of the town.

Headteachers at all eight schools were approached to elicit their cooperation for this research. All eight agreed and a plan of investigation including planned methods for data collection was also drawn up. A professional journal was also kept as part of the plan.

Because it wasn't possible to interview all eighty-one teaching staff at the eight schools it was decided to distribute a questionnaire for them to complete. The plan was then to interview some of the Traveller children to gain their perspective on the situation and finally to interview some of the children's parents. By using this form of triangulation the interpretation of the situation would be more balanced. Questions to be used for an interview with the headteachers were sent out in advance and appointments were made for the interviews to take place.

Negotiations began during staff meetings at the eight schools. Jill spoke to the teaching staff, explained the research and handed out questionnaires. Where there were problems Jill arranged with the head teachers to explain the research, its code of practice and hand out the questionnaires to their staff. It was agreed to collect them a week later. This proved to be more of a problem than anticipated. It took more than a week and in some cases up to three weeks to get the questionnaires back. One school opted out.

Permission was obtained from the children's parents and only children who were prepared to participate were interviewed. It was decided that the most appropriate way to approach the subject with the children was to firstly share some of the books now available about Traveller culture and then tape record an interview. The boys and girls interviewed ranged in age from 7 to 12. Several children scheduled for interview left the area just as the study began. The children were interviewed at their respective schools in a quiet room away from the classroom, with the exception of one who was interviewed at home in the presence of her mother.

It was agreed that all participants would remain anonymous. Any comments made by any of them would not be shared with any other participant and would remain confidential. It was also agreed with the participants that they would not be identified in the writing up of the research and a code of practice was agreed with them.

Interviews with headteachers

The first headteacher to be interviewed said that after receiving the copy of the questions to be asked, he was not prepared to give a taped interview. He presented Jill with a school prospectus, a copy of the schools' Shared Values Policy and her paper of questions with additional notes. A brief discussion followed, in the school entrance hall. Jill left feeling a little let down. The remainder of the headteacher interviews were more satisfactory.

When asked if the schools had a written multicultural or equal opportunities policy only three of the eight were able to produce a copy of their equal opportunities policy. The other headteachers said it was being incorporated in other school policies or that it was out of date and needed rewriting. When asked about the ways in which schools reflected the cultures of the children attending the schools, the common response was that they recognised the cultures of all ethnic groups by celebrating festivals and including studies of other cultures in parts of the curriculum. One headteacher said:

It is something we have worked hard at both formally and informally so things are written into, for example our Religious Education curriculum, giving lots of scope for our Muslim children to share their religion etc. because this is the largest group. We do a lot of looking at other peoples traditions, artefacts, festivals, both in assemblies and in classes. More than that I think it's the informal bits of it whereby we have a school culture. We live it in all that we do.

It became clear that three schools relied heavily on the support of the Ethnic Minority Support Service for input to the school. When asked specifically about including Traveller culture in things that went on in the school, two of the headteachers openly admitted that they had never done so. One of these schools had only recently taken in Traveller children and the other had never had any. One headteacher said that Traveller culture was included in the school but when asked to give some examples answered in vague terms. Another headteacher did not appear to understand the question and talked about Travellers 'fitting in and not being able to pick them out'. Another talked in terms of including trailers in a topic about homes. The headteachers at both these schools felt it was something that they should do but that 'it was a culture which is harder to know about'. They felt that there would be some 'consumer resistance' to its introduction in the school. Both said that they felt they would need help and advice with the introduction of Traveller culture into their respective schools, as they did not know enough about it. These were both schools which had no Traveller children on roll.

In answer to the question about schools ensuring that the teaching staff were made aware of Traveller culture, one headteacher avoided the question completely by talking about resources, and another said that it 'was a weak area and was not done as strongly as it could be'. He said that it had not been discussed as an issue with staff and not an area they had focused on. Only one headteacher said that Traveller culture was part of the planning of the school and that teaching staff were very aware of this group of children.

The final question was about resources in the schools specifically about Traveller culture. All the headteachers said that they had no resources or only a few books in the school library that reflected Traveller culture in any way but all said they would like to include more books of this kind in their school. One headteacher was not aware that any books about Travellers were available and 'would love to know of any'. Even though there were no Traveller children in her school she felt that having overheard derogatory remarks about Travellers by parents and one of the school governors, she would like to counteract the situation. She had had Traveller children at her previous school and would welcome new Traveller books and would make a point of using them.

Seven of the eight headteachers admitted that Traveller culture was not reflected in their schools but most were prepared to consider its inclusion. They were eager to know about new resources and their use in schools.

Teacher Questionnaires

The overall return of questionnaires was 28 per cent, with one school returning 100 per cent and another returning none. All the schools had an equal opportunities policy but only 74 per cent said it did include Traveller children and others said it did not specify. One respondent was not sure and another said that it was council policy. When asked to give a demonstration example, 70 per cent could not and, of the others, one said that the school 'SEN policy sets out educational provision for Traveller pupils and meeting their needs'. This implied that all Traveller children had special educational needs, which is not the case. The others expressed similar views along the lines of 'all children should be treated the same and are expected to follow the same rules and routines'.

When asked to say in what way the school reflected the cultures of the children attending the school 65 per cent responded with answers linked to stories, festivals, assemblies, cross-curricular elements, religious education, language around the building and books in the library. Twenty two per cent made no response and one commented that the school had input from the Ethnic Minority Support Service.

When asked how they reflected Traveller culture in their classrooms, 52 per cent made no response and 39 per cent said that they included it in topic work, discussion, books and posters in the classroom. One responded with the comment that 'curriculum guidelines are very structured therefore making it difficult to include their culture', another said that 'school life and timetables are very structured so it is difficult to truly reflect their culture'.

The questionnaire went on to ask in what ways could they include Traveller culture in their classrooms, if they didn't already. Almost half the respondents declined to answer and 13 per cent said that they didn't feel they knew enough themselves and needed more information about Traveller culture, while 35 per cent said they would use stories, artefacts, books and discussion. One responded that because she had a small resource base as a teaching area all her resources were based on the literacy hour. One teacher responded that she would use books like *Famous Five* and *Wind in the Willows.*

When asked about specific resources in the schools, almost half responded that there were none in the school about Travellers while more than half said the school had some but they were 'out of date' or they 'only had two books'. One respondent noted that the school had resources but these were borrowed from the TESS.

We asked those who said they had such resources in their classrooms whether they had used them. Forty one per cent made no response, 16 per cent said 'never', 8 per cent said that it was not being covered in the curriculum in year groups being taught, and a further 8 per cent said they were new to the school. The remaining 27 per cent said that they had used the resources in group discussions, humanities, at story time and as templates illustrating time lines.

The questionnaire went on to ask if they thought they had sufficient access to information about Traveller culture to support them in their classrooms. Almost two thirds answered no, 8 per cent made no response and of the remaining one third two said that they would like more information and one that 'all children were treated as equals and equally valued'. A further two said that it was not an issue in their school as there were no Traveller children, and one said she had had support from TESS.

The final question was where would they as teachers go to acquire further information? Twenty six per cent made no response, 17 per cent responded that they didn't know and the remaining 44 per cent said they would contact the Traveller Education Support Service and one even said she would telephone the researcher. Of this 44 per cent, the majority were from the sample schools who had Traveller children on roll. One responded they had no idea but would ring their multicultural resources centre for advice if it became an issue, while another responded that they would contact the LEA Council Equal Opportunities Officer. One said that she felt Traveller children needed their own teaching unit which could give them the culture and flexibility they need. Her school only had Traveller children for brief periods in the Summer term, when families camped in the area of the school.

Interviews with Children

Before beginning the interviews with the children Jill explained what she was doing in the research and that the children would be given the opportunity to listen to the recording after their interview. She wanted to know from them what they thought about the books they were shown.

After sharing the books the taped interviews began. The children were asked what they thought of the books. Some were reticent and some made no response of any kind. One child shrugged her shoulders and said 'I don't know'. The children who responded openly were very curious about the books and wanted to know why they were about Travellers. One child asked 'where did you get them from and why have you got them?' One said that the books had 'lots of colour and stuff' but thought some of the non-fiction books were dull because they only have black and white pictures, but that the information is interesting. The overall comment from the children was that the books were alright or good. When asked what they liked or disliked about them they were happy with the contents of the books and thought them funny, adventurous and interesting. The pop-up book was a particular favourite, even with the older children who commented that younger siblings would probably enjoy them. One child said that she liked the stories but didn't like the books because 'they used Travellers, they shouldn't use Travellers because it's a bit upsetting'. Her sister said that she liked the books 'because they were about Travellers and I am a Traveller'. The older children commented that some of the books were too young for them but they would like similar books for their own age group. One said 'my little sister would love me to read the mammoth story to her'. There was nothing that the children particularly disliked about the books.

Three quarters of the children had never seen any books about Travellers before, in their current school or elsewhere. A third of them had seen a few books at a previous school in a different area, but not at their current school. When asked whether they would like to have books like these in their schools, all but one of the children were positive. One qualified: 'yes if they are interesting'. One was unhappy about such books being part of the school, 'because everyone will take the mickey out of me'.

Two thirds of the children thought that other children in their school would like to see books about Travellers. The rest were unsure and a small number said no. When asked if they would like stories about Travellers shared in their classroom, maybe in literacy hour, the majority said 'yes', and one said 'yes, so people know about how Travellers live'. A small number said 'no' they would not like such stories to be read or be in the classroom. Several of the children were reluctant to answer the question and preferred responding with nods.

Interviews with parents
Even though parents had agreed to be interviewed and wanted to co-operate fully they were nervous about being taped and the way they would come over on the tape. Confidentiality was assured but one parent requested that the tape be destroyed after use. All the parents were given the list of the questions in advance and questions were read and clarified when necessary. One parent was so concerned about what the interview was for, who else would hear the tape, and whether it was for any officials, that an hour of discussion was needed before the interview could begin. Much of what was said during the discussion was of more value than the interview as it revealed a great deal, not just about her views on education but about society.

Parents were asked if they thought the schools their children attended were interested in the Traveller way of life. They all responded that they didn't think the schools were in any way interested in their way of life. We asked them how they could tell and the parents offered evidence for their views. One said 'I have never seen them bring home anything about Travellers', and another said, 'well I can't say how I know but as far as I know at the moment then no'.

They were unanimous that they had never seen anything brought home from school about Traveller life and several wanted to know why not. One parent thought that schools should have books about Travellers and said, 'I think they should because we live in this community where there are lots of Travellers around. We are Travellers and our children should know about our life. They are the new generation'.

With regard to the school curriculum and focus on Travellers in school, half the parents felt that it was not important because they could teach their children all that they needed to know about their own way of life and that the 'country people' might teach them the wrong things. The other half thought it was very important. One said 'our children are part of the school as well and they should have something of them in the school. I would like all country generations to learn about Travellers. My children mix with them and we live in this community and they know we are Travellers, We are not ashamed'. Another parent was more ambiguous, 'it all depends what they are trying to learn. Not just that it's a one way thing with Travellers. They mix it up with other nationalities then I wouldn't mind that'.

Parents wanted the true history of Travellers to be taught, because they said, 'there will always be Travellers whether they live in a house or on a site'. One parent related how her grandfather had fought in the First World War and she had seen photographs of him in a book about his regiment. She also felt that there should be documentaries and films made about Travellers and their way of life that could be used in schools so that the children could learn the truth about Travellers.

Some parents spoke about the prejudice Travellers faced. One declared that 'the first thing they should learn about Travellers is racism for one, and to speak on the good side and the bad side of Travellers'. In their own experiences at school, only bad things were ever said to Travellers.

When parents were asked whether they would be prepared to go into the schools and talk to teachers and pupils about their way of life, many didn't understand what exactly we meant. Their responses were mixed. Half the group were hesitant and weren't sure how effective it would be. One parent observed that, 'I wouldn't say that it would make a difference if I did speak about Travellers. One school won't make a difference unless a lot of schools get involved in it as well'. The other half were more positive and would welcome the opportunity to go into the schools and talk about their way of life but were not sure that the schools would invite them.

One of the parents commented on the fact that his eldest child was now at secondary school, which made him very proud as he himself never went any further than primary school. Another parent stated that the children were sent to school only because they had to and not because they really wanted them to attend.

From interpreting the responses of all the participants in this research, there appears to be a serious omission of Traveller culture in schools, for three reasons. Firstly the schools admitted that they didn't reflect the culture of Traveller children, whether there were Traveller children attending the schools or not. The headteachers felt that it was not an area of work that they felt confident about because of their lack of knowledge of the culture. The headteachers who said that they did include Traveller awareness in the school were rather vague about how it was done or said it was included in a topic about homes (with stereotypical trailers). The teachers were more negative: either they didn't include Traveller culture or they didn't see the need to include Traveller culture, particularly when Traveller children already attended their schools. Those who did include Traveller culture did so in the same home-is-a-trailer stereotypical manner. The lack of school resources related to Traveller culture made it clear that it was not a priority in the school curriculum. This was confirmed further by the school library service which had no specific Traveller books and had never had a request for any.

Secondly the children confirmed that the schools had no resources that reflected Traveller culture and had no opportunity to talk about their way of life in the normal course of events in the classroom. The children had never seen books in school about themselves. Does this reflect how they were valued in the schools? The data demonstrated that one child wanted to keep her identity as a Traveller hidden from the other children as much as possible because of her feelings about being a Traveller in school or possibly because of her fear of the consequences of other children knowing. If every child needs to feel individually valued to enable them to succeed in school it follows that Traveller children need to feel valued for who they are in the same way as other children regardless of their race, culture or religion.

Thirdly the parents saw that although their children attended local schools, the schools were not interested in their way of life. Their children were living in the local community and yet the schools didn't acknowledge their contribution to that community.

The schools said that they reflected the cultures of other ethnic groups of pupils but these groups did not include Travellers.

The Ofsted report, *Raising the Attainment of Minority Ethnic Pupils* clearly states, 'Gypsy Traveller pupils are the group most at risk in the education system' (Ofsted, 1999). What were these schools doing to raise the children's attainment? To raise any child's attainment their self-esteem also has to be raised, so Traveller children need to feel valued in the same way as other children. This can only be done if each child is recognised for who they are, and sees this reflected in the school environment (Davis, 1986). This is equally true for Traveller children (Holmes, 1993).

As far back as 1980 it was recognised that good education was based not on one culture but on valuing diversity (DES, 1980). Many subsequent reports (Swann, 1985 and Ofsted, 1996) have concluded that the inappropriateness and inflexibility of the education system, together with racism, discrimination, and stereotyping have a great influence on the education of children (Brown, 1998). To advance in any meaningful way schools must take on board the recommendation that in order to reflect the needs of a diverse society schools must value cultural diversity (Macpherson, 1999).

As a result of this research at least two of the schools have invited Jill to speak at staff meetings about Traveller issues. She is also working with the school library service to compile a comprehensive list of Traveller books to recommend for schools. Professional Development/INSET with Traveller parent input is to be included in future TESS plans. Although it was clear at the outset of the investigation that many of the schools in the LEA didn't reflect Traveller culture, it wasn't realised how extensive the problem was and how much work still needed to be done.

2. Traveller education as equality education

Trish has worked for a local authority TESS for three years. The TESS seeks to bring about long term, sustainable change in schools, the LEA and the wider society through multicultural education within mainstream society so that settled and Traveller communities would come to understand more about each other.

For the purpose of this case story, Travellers included English or Welsh Gypsies, Irish or Scottish Travellers together with Showmen, Circus, Bargee and New Travellers. Gypsy Travellers are a recognised ethnic group and those Travellers of Irish origin also have ethnic status.

This AR was planned as a step by step process over a period of time which was monitored, reflected upon, modified evaluated and brought about directional change to the researcher's practice and understanding. The overall aim was to bring about an improvement of the situation and practice of the practitioner-researcher (O'Hanlon, 1999).

The purpose of the AR was to make an audit of the TESS role in the promotion of multicultural education for Travellers, and the part played by the LEA and schools. Data was gathered from members of TESS, headteachers and teachers by means of questionnaires, interviews and journal entries. Service documentation including policy statement, service statement, leaflets sent into schools and job descriptions were reviewed to see if the promotion of culture specific materials in the learning process in schools was being identified. As part of the audit, stock was taken of all the resources such as books, videos and artefacts so that items could be catalogued and stored appropriately, and any gaps in provision noted. The plan was to get a wider understanding of where the TESS role fitted into the LEA's policy and practice in this area.

The investigation lasted for six months and focused on the recognition of Traveller culture within multicultural education and the TESS's role in promoting it. The question set for the research was:

'What does TESS do to promote multicultural education for Travellers in schools and what does it need to do?'

The data collected was mainly qualitative and interpretative with some additional statistical and factual information. Much of it was subjective, eliciting opinions and viewpoints so was possibly liable to bias, so triangulation was used to cross-check the findings during the course of the research. Data had been gathered from a number of sources such as schools, particularly headteachers, individual teachers and TESS colleagues to provide balance. At times, colleagues in mainstream teaching, the TESS and family acted as critical friends with regard to the data and its interpretation. Their questions and responses helped to clarify thoughts and refine the work in terms of the data, methodology and interpretation.

Trish kept a journal-diary. Holly (1989) commends this as an effective way for teachers to analyse practice. Some entries were of chronological events; others reported meetings, observations, opinions and reflections. Many of the journal entries were also written on pieces of paper and secreted away. Thus, the whole AR process enabled reflection and self-evaluation.

The other methods of data collection were questionnaires and interviews. A code of practice was drawn up and although it was not sent out with the questionnaires, interviewees and those filling in the evaluation sheet were verbally informed of the code. The goodwill of the participants was vital to the research so a flexible and open approach was essential.

This AR did not lend itself to a tight structure. The informal interviews were open-ended with permission for notes to be taken but the more formal interviews took place with headteachers. One such interview was taped with the consent of the interviewee and a copy of the questions sent beforehand. The second interviewee did not wish to see the questions and there was no time to organise a tape recorder.

The other means of data collection was the questionnaire. It was originally intended to send a questionnaire to a limited number of schools. Previous experience had shown that questionnaires were difficult to construct. There were problems with the number, design and construction of appropriate questions and piloting the questions, as well as their distribution and return.

However, the research project coincided with the distribution of the Traveller Awareness Pack (TAP) that TESS had compiled to go into all schools. An evaluation sheet was included, with questions modified to include additional data for the project. The evaluation sheet was based on one used in another LEA support service which had yielded a 50 per cent return. The questions were modified, checked, trialled and validated by TESS colleagues. Some questions required yes or no responses, others an open-ended response. The evaluation sheet was sent out in the TAP which included a freepost, internal mail return address.

A more structured evaluation questionnaire was also used in schools where the TESS undertook multicultural work. In most cases these were filled in on the spot so that they could immediately be taken away.

The journal began with an initial response to what TESS was doing to promote multicultural education for Travellers in schools. This was developed to consider what the service could do to include Traveller culture and lifestyle in the curriculum of local schools. Although Traveller children did not often have their culture or ethnicity respected, implicit in the research question was the principle that multicultural education must be a two way process.

The audit of the service focused on all the physical resources held by TESS. Many of the resources had a strong cultural bias and could be described as 'display' items. The service also had a selection of videos and tapes and books for children and adults. The display items were used for teaching and learning purposes, as were a range of other learning support games, jigsaws and reading scheme books. Some items may not have had a direct, obvious cultural link to Travellers but were often used with Traveller children to help them understand aspects of mainstream culture e.g. small toys relating to a house, a hospital, the dentist.

As a result of the research, the resources have been catalogued and stored more appropriately, and a current list of display items and books has been circulated to all schools. There are also plans to post the list on the LEA schools' website.

Display resources were the main contribution to multicultural education (apart from the TESS staff) and resources and displays encouraged interest, motivation and raised awareness. Although these material items were not seen as the culture itself, they were used to encourage schools and pupils to use and interpret them in an appropriate cultural context. Thus, the materials used for display had to be shown as the group would have liked to see them (Grant *et al*, 1989; Bullivant, 1989; Holmes, 1993). Display materials were also taken into schools and their uses discussed with staff to raise awareness and promote a positive image of Travellers.

Informal interviews were held with two colleagues, an educational welfare officer and a teacher. The question asked was 'What is the Service doing to promote multicultural education, for Traveller children, and what else could be done?'. Their responses reflected their professional interest and particular perspective. There was also a difference in enthusiasm about the issue, with one colleague clearly taking on board the notion of multicultural education while the other was more cautious and appeared to provide safe answers. Interviewees frequently focused on the practices in one school rather than taking an LEA perspective. They agreed to fill in a questionnaire designed around the research question and had a week before a staff meeting to complete it for discussion.

After tabulation of the questionnaire responses from local schools and colleagues, the key issues that emerged were:

• the service seldom took culturally specific resources into schools, either for all children or Traveller children

• the display resources were not well used or seen. Out of 167 schools in the LEA only nine schools had used Traveller cultural materials in the last three years. During that period the service had worked to support children in 20 different schools

• all teaching staff agreed that it was an important part of the work and identified as such in most TESS documentation

• the service had no systematic way of monitoring input on Traveller cultural issues

• there were gaps in resources

- staff sought more books depicting Traveller culture and display equipment appropriate for use by secondary pupils and Bargees.

It was important that these resources were not used to reinforce stereotypes or create new ones or to emphasise differences when the aim is inclusion, but that they were used to help children take pride in their own culture and show Travellers in a positive light. Correspondence and informal discussions with the Assistant Chief Education Officer (Curriculum) have also been taking place and positive progress is being made. The Chief Education Officer has been supportive of the work of TESS and wrote a letter of commendation to go in the Traveller Awareness Pack.

A copy of the department's equal opportunities policy has been obtained. No reference is made to culture or Travellers but it seeks to support equal opportunities for everyone and entitlement to a good education for all, regardless of class, social circumstance, gender, disability or race. Reference is also made to the authority's determination not to tolerate harassment, stereotyping, bias and prejudice which encapsulates the issues which multicultural education wishes to address and the items the Macpherson Report (1999) believes education could support.

The Service sent a Traveller Awareness Pack to all 167 schools in the LEA during the summer term. It consisted of three information booklets (curriculum, school information, and a historical and cultural perspective), a set of photographs of some local Travellers and a published book of stories and memories told by local Travellers. An evaluation sheet was included in the pack and it was adapted to accommodate the research being carried out. It sought responses to the TAP as a multicultural resource and responses to the services offered to schools in the field of multicultural education.

Interpretation of results

- all respondents thought that the pack was good or excellent, provided a quality resource and a well-balanced approach, and looked highly professional

- 85 per cent thought it interesting and relevant, using phrases such as 'useful, informative and comprehensive; relevant to studies on minority groups; gave me a new perspective on issues and how this impacts on their time in school'

- One quarter of headteachers had not shown it to staff or staff had not had a chance to look at it. Two related on the telephone how it was located in the headteacher's room and that they chose to show it to the staff when appropriate. They found they had too many other things on their agenda

- many found it interesting but questioned the relevance since no Traveller children were on roll

- almost all agreed that the pack provided information about Traveller culture. One comment was 'you don't know what you don't know', which perhaps covered a number of respondents' thoughts

- a number admitted that it was an area that they had not thought of and one school felt that it was not an issue within the school. Some of the schools that answered in this way regularly had illegal encampments within their community and one local councillor was active in highlighting what he called the 'problem'

- a multicultural resource? Three quarters of the respondents agreed that items within the pack would be useful as a school or classroom resource. Some identified collective worship as a possible use for the material. A quarter were unable to answer the question accurately mainly because it had not been passed on to staff or it was 'too early in the year to say'

- one hundred per cent responded that the school did not have any multicultural resources that addressed the issue of Travellers. Two schools requested help in acquiring resources

- the question relating to the borrowing of Traveller culture resources elicited over a half of repondents' positive response. Three noted that they would like resources occasionally, although not at present, and one felt that they would be useful in Personal Social and Health Education (PSHE) or a religious education context.

- 62 per cent responded that they didn't need any additional information but three added that additional information was not required at present. One felt that information and training might only be needed when Traveller children were admitted to school. The remaining 38 per cent agreed that additional information was always useful

- 70 per cent responded that no staff training was needed, while those who said it was qualified their request in terms of uncertainty of time scale and 'in light of the staff's training workload'

- more than half of the respondents did not have Traveller children on roll, nor indeed had they ever knowingly had any. Two schools had Fairground children and one is located where traditionally most winter based Showmen children attend. The four other schools have, or have had, housed traditional Travellers. They have all been of Gypsy and English origin, although, as mentioned earlier, the schools did not identify the children as Gypsy.

There was some evidence that not all information which arrived in school was passed on to staff. One respondent had shown it to the senior management team but other headteachers, aware of the great workload on teachers, chose not to add more pressure on staff. TESS was aware of the huge pressures on school staff and felt this may also have contributed to the poor return rate of questionnaires and take up of training, information and resource loan. However, while headteachers may regulate information passed on to staff, all teachers have a responsibility to create and develop multicultural education in school.

A number of respondents indicated that they found the pack interesting but implied that it was not really relevant to their school because theirs had no Traveller children. This all-white-school response may be likened to other multicultural, multi-ethnic initiatives involving black children where predominantly white schools felt that multicultural education did not apply to them. Brandt (1986), Brown (1998), and the Swann Reports (DES, 1985) noted that 'all-white schools' were reluctant to address or incorporate issues relating to cultural diversity and racism but as Marsh (1999) comments these are the very schools where need may be greatest. Clarke (1998) believes TESS has a role to tackle the ignorance many people have about the life and culture of Traveller children as fear and prejudice can develop unless this ignorance is addressed. The children in our schools may encounter a range of Travelling people in the course of their lives and all schools have a responsibility to represent the Traveller culture positively in the curriculum for all children (DfEE, 1998).

All those who responded to the questionnaire indicated that they had no resources to reflect Traveller culture: no artefacts, books, fiction or non-fiction, audio or videotapes, photographs, software packages or worksheets. It could be argued that schools perpetuate negative attitudes to other cultures and races by not having such materials available for every child to use. Pupils from ethnic minority groups may feel that their culture and lifestyle is rejected and that this can lead to exclusions and truancy (NATT, 1998). Government departments are increasingly recognising the value of resources that reflect various cultures and ethnic groups in promoting all round development and achievement (DfEE, 1998; Ofsted, 1996, 1998). In 1996 Ofsted commented that in those schools that celebrated the different Travelling groups with positive images the response of the pupils was good. In schools where Traveller children were incognito the pupils responded less well. In *Raising the Achievement of Minority Ethnic Pupils* (Ofsted, 1999) it was noted that many of the schools surveyed celebrated the cultural and ethnic diversity reflected in the school but seemed reluctant to do so with regard to Traveller culture. Such reluctance means schools are failing to help all of their children to reach their full potential. According to Banks (1989), 'students learn best and are highly motivated when their school curriculum reflects their cultures, experiences and perspectives'.

Some schools indicated that they would welcome additional information about Traveller lifestyle and culture. These schools supported the importance of knowing as much as possible about the different groups they taught or the pupils they were likely to encounter. Only through knowledge of other cultures can teachers respect minority groups and not make value judgements about culturally different groups (Bullivant, 1989; Brown, 1998). There was concern, however, that the majority of respondents did not request additional information. It was hoped that the Traveller Awareness Pack would stimulate a thirst to access more information about Traveller life and culture.

Teachers were urged to ensure that the curriculum should reflect today's multicultural society, particularly in subject areas (ATL, 1999; Ofsted, 1995, 1996; NATT, 1998; TTA, 1998). It is only when multicultural perspectives are embedded into the curriculum and structures of school that the issue of equal opportunities is really addressed (Ivatts, 1999).

Given the pressure that schools are now under from government initiatives many of these issues may not be considered. However, Marsh (1999) urges schools to look at the whole curriculum from a global multicultural, multiethnic perspective, and Davis (1986) notes that while education alone cannot compensate for society's wrongs with regards to racism it must work towards tackling it.

Heavy workload appeared to be the main reason for the limited requests for additional information, possibly because research about Travellers and their schooling is not yet a priority in schools.

Headteacher Interviews
The then CES has highlighted that 'headteachers must take the leading role in ensuring the quality of curricular provision' (DES, 1992 p46). Two headteachers were interviewed. They were chosen because their schools have Traveller children on a regular basis. For more than a generation school A has admitted traditional Travellers (settled and transient) from the council caravan site. School B had recently taken Travellers, and although the numbers were small, the population was mixed. There were traditional Travellers in houses and from an illegal but tolerated private site; there were occasionally highly mobile children from illegal encampments and there were Showmen children who used it as a winter base school. Both head teachers were men who had been appointed within the last three years. Headteacher B had no previous experience of working with Traveller children but headteacher A had spent much of his teaching associated with Travellers in his present school.

Headteacher A agreed to an interview immediately, following a request for an appointment. He did not wish to see the questions and the interview was not taped but notes were taken. A copy of the questionnaire was given in advance to headteacher B and his responses were taped. Headteacher B showed great enthusiasm towards Travellers. He welcomed TESS resources, displayed them centrally in a high profile way and was open to further suggestions about improving information and children's knowledge of Travellers. Traveller culture was becoming more of an issue for the school because the school had recently enrolled a high number of Traveller children.

Headteacher A remembered the time when TESS and the staff were based in the school and took all the responsibility for the Traveller children. He didn't seem to be aware of what was happening in the classrooms, particularly with regard to multicultural education and curriculum content. There was also a sense that although Travellers made up 10 to 20 percent of the school population, the headteacher didn't wish their differences to be highlighted, suggesting again an incognito status (Ofsted, 1996 p18).

School A had a high proportion of children of Asian origin but the Ethnic Minority Support Service staff took responsibility for any displays. There was curriculum coverage in geography (a study of Pakistan) and RE (Islam). This school wished to treat all the children the same and ignored the differences which made the children unique individuals. It seemed that by ignoring the child's own culture and associated experiences the school was denying the opportunity to use these children and their culture as a valuable resource (Brown, 1998 and Holmes, 1997).

If significant change is to occur in multicultural education the principles and practice needed to be embedded in the curriculum. Ofsted (1999) noted that primary schools in particular were reluctant to use the Programmes of study to help them address the issue of pupil cultural background. Many of the reported schools felt that this was patronising. But ignoring the culture of different ethnic and cultural groups can have serious negative consequences not only for the ethnic groups concerned but also for mainstream society. It is the responsibility of the headteacher and senior management to take a strong lead to address these issues (NATT, 1998; TTA, 1998).

School policies

School B did not have a school policy relating to equal opportunities, although equal opportunities were mentioned in the main school policy. There was no written multicultural policy although the headteacher felt the school did practise multiculturalism. School A had an equal opportunity policy that had an antiracist element. The headteacher said that Travellers were not specifically mentioned but that the policy applied to all children.

According to Ofsted, schools with strong equal opportunity policies and which celebrated cultural diversity were the schools where Traveller children were valued and appeared to achieve higher standards (Ofsted, 1996). The quality of opportunity offered to different groups of pupils is more important than aiming for the same opportunities for all pupils yet 'this is not necessarily equality of opportunity' (Gay, 1989).

Ethnicity

Both headteachers recognised Gypsies as an ethnic minority and felt that in principle their culture and lifestyle should be incorporated in the curriculum. School B was handling this at the level of 'saris and samosas' by having displays and story reading from TESS. School A featured Travellers within a homes topic. Every child had their home visited and photographs taken outside their door but much depended on the presence of a Traveller child and the willingness of the teacher to visit. In the last three years this school has not requested display resources to support the topic.

Clearly, neither pupils nor teachers could leave their cultural background at home and the sharing and celebrating of differences which can help encourage cultural awareness and multicultural education are yet to be fully developed. Until schools move from displays or adds towards integration in curriculum planning and the inclusion of topics and issues deliberately viewed from diverse perspectives, various cultural or ethnic groups including Travellers will not be fully represented in the curriculum or the school.

Resources

Neither school had resource material that reflected Traveller culture. A survey of both schools' library shelves revealed little, but one teacher in school A thought they had a copy of Josie Patterson's *Traveller Child*. School B acknowledged that they had the Traveller Awareness Pack for use. Headteacher B thought that they ought to get more resources, particularly if they were to regularly get Traveller children, but headteacher A indicated that it was not in his plans to resource this aspect of school life. When challenged over the issue of display and resources for Traveller culture he admitted that there were no displays in his school but added that neither were there any reflecting any other ethnic minority group! It seemed that in spite of having Traveller children on roll these two schools are yet to become inclusive schools, that fully reflect their multicultural intake.

Both schools used TESS as learning support for Traveller children. School B also used TESS for resources loans, story reading, information, informal training and liaison. However, school A had not made use of TESS cultural resources and school staff requests had always been for non-Traveller cultural materials such as reading scheme books, or requests for toys broken by Traveller children.

Although the TESS co-ordinator and headteacher A have now arranged half-termly meetings where a resource loan service is offered, and also training, its success depends on the schools themselves requesting resources, staff training and visits.

Self-esteem

Good teachers are aware of the link between pupils' high self-esteem and learning progress. So a welcoming school which values children's culture and a positive teacher attitude and approach can help raise pupil self-esteem (Phillips, 1994). Both headteachers acknowledged a positive link between displaying Traveller culturally-related items and Traveller children's self-esteem. Headteacher A wanted children to bring culturally-related items into school and felt that these could be displayed in the classroom rather than taken to a remote school display. He didn't think it was a question of the school providing items for display in acknowledgement or recognition of a specific cultural group like Travellers.

Headteacher B saw the connection between displaying artefacts and children's self-esteem but said cautiously that 'it can go either way'. He recognised that some Traveller children didn't wish to be identified as, or associated with, Travellers for a variety of reasons such as fear of prejudice or victimisation. The school had displayed Traveller items in central locations and they had prompted much interest among children, teachers, parents and visitors. However, he could not recall any of the Traveller children making themselves known as expert about Traveller items on display.

The role of TESS
Both head teachers found the service resources accessible. However, both highlighted the need for the service to be the provider and deliverer of the items. Staff could arrange the displays but the time and workload pressures on school staff would make it likely that staff would be unable and unwilling to collect goods.

Headteacher B also distinguished between the physical resources and the human resources, believing both were valuable in helping schools and staff to work towards more inclusive multicultural education. Headteacher A thought that the service could do all kinds of things to help the school in the field of multicultural education and qualified this in terms of input into class and group work, collective worship and staff INSET, but then added hastily: 'but in practical terms we are booked up'.

In summary:
- some schools, while recognising the ethnicity of some Travellers, did not acknowledge or celebrate their culture

- school policies and practices did not always address multi-cultural issues

- there was a lack of curriculum coverage of Traveller life and culture

- there was a lack of school-based resources that reflected Traveller culture, particularly in schools that regularly admitted Travellers

- TESS cultural resources were seen as a good thing, particularly if they were delivered to school by a member of TESS staff, thus enabling information, informal training and liaison to take place.

The investigation set out to address the question 'What does the TESS do to promote multicultural education for Travellers in schools and what does it need to do?' The project investigated physical resources, documentation and the opinions of TESS staff, schoolteachers and headteachers.

This investigation provided only a snapshot of the views and situation in one LEA's schools. However, information acquired offered some answers to the question as well as indications of what the service needs. TESS actively promotes multicultural education for Travellers both in schools and in the community. Some progress was achieved, particularly by the education welfare officers and TESS staff, in increasing their contacts with parents. The main focus of the Services' multicultural educational work was through display and events such as book week. Some culturally specific material was used with Traveller children but the service needed to make these more widely available to teachers and other children. There was also no monitoring of schools' curriculum input regarding multicultural resources.

Display is the simplest and probably the most effective means of ensuring that Traveller culture is included as multicultural education. However, the number of schools that TESS had loaned materials to was small. Many schools indicated that they would like more display resources. Schools were willing to borrow the free resources but wanted them delivered to school by TESS staff so that there could be personal support and input, and additional incidental staff training.

Some schools had an unplanned approach to multicultural and Traveller education covering the topic if it arose rather than pre-planning a genuine multicultural curriculum in spite of National Curriculum overload.

Many of the schools took the view that Traveller education was not an issue until the Traveller children actually arrived at the school. The investigation reaffirms the role of TESS staff in their work with all schools, encouraging them to take steps to affirm Gypsy and Traveller cultures.

Curriculum

TESS has raised the issue of Traveller culture across the authority with their Traveller Awareness Pack. The schools that have taken it on board are operating at what Banks (1989 p193) calls Level 1 Contribution Approach, where cultural artefacts are introduced into the curriculum as 'add ons', using what he described as the saris and samosas approach. Indeed, TESS have encouraged this approach for two reasons. It is perhaps the introductory level for schools that have not yet acknowledged Travellers as part of the multicultural and multi-ethnic continuum. Secondly, TESS can have more control at this stage, as higher levels of incorporating multicultural education into the curriculum require a change from within the school itself. The change has to be in the taught curriculum, resources, management and pedagogy and also in the hidden curriculum (ethos and attitude). TESS can help schools through these levels but the impetus for help and support needs to come from within the school. Multicultural education is not just about changing the curriculum, it is a long-term process and not a quick solution for the occasional Traveller child who may enrol.

It is hoped that in future, issues of multicultural education may become more significant in the curriculum of schools. The Macpherson Report (Home Office, 1999) and the promotion of citizenship (DfEE, 1997) aim to make everyone feel that they have a stake in our society and the community. Traveller children need to feel part of the community and it is the role of education to address cultural issues and engage all minority groups, giving them positive learning experiences. Schools must, however, be seen to be fair to all students because it is possible that changes made without careful thought might alienate the majority of mainstream pupils.

The action research project was difficult to develop in an authority that had little multicultural work generated at LEA level, there was no adviser with responsibility for multicultural education, and the Ethnic Minority Support Service did little on issues of equality and social inclusion. Little research material about Travellers existed and most references to multicultural education related to other ethnic minorities.

The research methods chosen created difficulties. There were problems getting questionnaires returned but the information in those that were returned was valuable. The interviews took time to arrange and were dependent upon the use of other people's time and good will. However the research confirmed the view that TESS and schools have different priorities. Education for social inclusion is a priority for TESS yet it appears to be less so for schools.

The investigation has provided TESS with information from a number of schools interested in receiving display resources, information and training. It has also provided the foundation for an action plan which will enable the service to constructively move forward to promote more widespread inclusive education in LEA schools for all its pupils.

3. Is Traveller language used in school?

John has personally experienced the prejudice felt about Travellers through his friendship and collaboration with Travelling people. These associations have led him to take up employment supporting Traveller children in school and he is strongly committed to their education. So he was highly motivated to play a part in making schooling for Traveller children as pleasurable and worthwhile as possible while counteracting any discrimination against them.

He wanted his action research to play a part in improving school practice and to influence educational reforms affecting Traveller children through professional development. He investigated the home language of Travelling families and the difference this might make to their schooling. He was aware that the language of Travelling communities was a real issue with regard to the schooling of their children, and writers in the field (Liegeois, 1998; Ivatts, 1998) have called for action research about this to be undertaken.

The research used taped interviews with people likely to shed light on the research question namely teachers, parents and pupils. This involved both professionals and their clients in the process thereby developing through collaborative reflection – what Elliott (1991) describes as 'the courage to critique the curriculum structure, which shapes their practices, and the power to negotiate change within the system that maintains them'. Key issues were examined as they appeared prior to and during the action research project.

John considered that Traveller language in school had largely been ignored in the UK. Although *The Resolution on School Provision for Gypsy and Traveller Children* (EU, 1989) led to new educational developments in the United Kingdom, the advice with regard to language has not been taken up. The resolution asked for research into language and suggested that language was a necessary part of an intellectual approach to education. Traveller language, like all languages, provides the core of their culture. Many European Gypsies are bilingual and their knowledge of the language of their domicile or host nation may be limited. Romany teachers were employed in schools in Europe. Yet in the UK the call for mother tongue speakers doesn't appear as an educational imperative. There is a dilemma amongst members of the Travelling communities because some would be glad were their language openly recognised in schools and teaching materials adapted accordingly, whereas other Travellers consider their language to be exclusive to themselves, a kind of secret language (Liegeois, 1998). The term 'language deprivation' was unjustifiably being applied to Traveller children, so enforcing the stereotype of an underclass. Even in schools with a relatively long history of educating Traveller children there was little awareness of specific aspects of their culture and particularly their language. This investigation and its interviews are confined to Romany Gypsies in order to focus the research on one specific Traveller community.

Visits were made to families and teachers prior to the formal interviews so as to find families and teachers who would be willing to take part, to outline the reasons for the research, its aims, and the nature of the questions to be asked. All participants were assured of confidentiality and were advised that an ethical code of practice would be used (see O'Hanlon, 2003). Interviews were to be informal.

A pilot interview was arranged with one group of Gypsies to test out the appropriateness of the interview questions and to find out whether they knew anyone who would agree to a taped interview.

This pilot went so well that the original families identified agreed to be interviewed and they confirmed the extensive use of the Romani language by Gypsy families. The Gypsies chosen for the investigation were: a grandfather Raf, his daughter Mary another mother Sal, grandmother Judy, and Mag a sixteen year old relative.

Raf knew the Romani language well, so well, he said, that he had no more to learn. He was adamant that he wouldn't use the language in the interview, partly because he considered this would be impolite, and because his belief was that the language was for Romany people themselves and would cause problems for them if *Gorjas* (non-Gypsy) got to understand their language. He had taken some time to learn it and it was not until he had reached his advanced age that he knew it well. He believed that children picked the language up straight away and it was important that they were encouraged to speak it. He said 'That's our way. We can tell our children to do something without others knowing what we are saying. You don't want everybody to know'.

Raf was appalled to hear that some Gypsy children used Romani in school. He didn't believe that this was right for their families. He was dismissive of the notion that using Romani in storybooks at school could be useful. He insisted that the language was not for sharing with other children. When asked if he thought the children understood the teachers, he replied 'we bring them up to understand, we bring them up that way. To be civil and respectful.'

His daughter Mary said she didn't know much Romani. Her children probably knew more than she did, having learnt it from their father. She felt that she knew as much of the language as she wanted to know. She thought that resources and classroom practices that reflected the Traveller culture were acceptable in school but she had the same attitude to language as her father. She insisted that it was wrong for children to use home language at school, that it was only for use at home. Teachers understood the children and wouldn't need to know any of their language.

Sal and Judy use Romani at home. Sal was very keen to know much more of the language. She is a young mother whose two children, age 4 and 5, attended the local school. Judy knew enough of the language to speak it fluently.

Judy recollected that her grandfather used to sit down and teach them the language. She recognised the similarities to some Indian languages and described how she understood some words she heard in Asian restaurants, and would have conversations with the restaurant staff about how alike their languages were. Sal and Judy both stated that Romani was very important to them and central to their life and culture. It was natural for them to encourage their children to speak it.

Some of the home language was used by the children at school, such as *mutta* (to go to the toilet). They thought it would be useful for teachers to understand basic words like *mutta*, because they thought that schooling could be very stressful for a child who speaks only Romani. 'We don't say wee but my child will use both words. Staff need to know', Sal said firmly. Judy had used Romani words with non-Travellers without realising what she'd done and thought it would be easy for a child to do the same in school, which would mean that the teacher wouldn't understand what they were saying or 'what they was on about'. When children's books specifically about Traveller life, like *Shaun's Wellies* and *A Horse for Joe* were discussed, the grandmother exclaimed 'a full story about Travellers! I'd feel funny! I'd think everyone was looking at me! I'd feel embarrassed only me and all these *Gorjas*!'

When asked what they thought about adapting activities like drawing a house to include drawing a caravan or trailer Judy thought it was wrong to make the children feel different. She protested, saying 'a child might want to draw a house, then they are told, No you draw a trailer! But you – you draw a trailer – wouldn't feel nice would you? Better if you have a choice. A different way of doing it. What would you like to do? Gives child options, doesn't make it feel pushed out to one side. People don't understand that children are just children and they're not different. A child has a child's mind. They should be tret the same, not thought of as you're a Traveller'.

This response indicates a different attitude in the younger generation of Gypsies about sharing Romani. When asked about the children using Romani in school they said they would discourage it, but made the proviso that it was useful in matters like toileting.

Judy explained 'like to keep the language to themselves, a culture we look to keep. We have been set aside for so long that we like to keep it that way. Settled or otherwise we still have the same values. Language is very important, one thing that will remain'.

The sixteen year old daughter Mag said she'd been 'fetched up with the language'. She had learned it from everybody in her community and had picked it up naturally. She used it in and away from home, indicating that secrecy was important and useful. She'd never used the language in written form at school, but used it a lot with her Gypsy peers in school. Mag had never thought of using Romani in her written work at school, but thought she might have enjoyed doing so. Her parents have never told her not to use Romani in school. She thought that 'they wouldn't be bothered whether she had or hadn't used it.' She thought children should know the proper word for toilet in school but still know the Romani word. Mag expressed passion about Romani and noted that, despite the majority of Gypsies now being housed, there has not been a demise of the language. 'It's still in your blood wherever you go. It's yours. A house can't change you. Our culture is like the blood in your body, it's your way of talking', she said.

Mag thought that the older Travellers were more entrenched in their views about language because 'they'd had the language longer than us. They'd not changed, they treasured the language'.

From these interviews it is evident that the Romani language is still very much alive among Gypsies today. It is learned from an early age. The younger mothers seemed to know some Romani but one was keen to know more while the other wasn't bothered. The grandparents however had an extensive knowledge of the language. Gypsies have an oral tradition learned naturally over many years from childhood onwards. Learning in school follows a different pattern, particularly with the prescriptive curriculum emphasis in schools today. Traveller children learn through an oral system that is educationally different from the emphasis in state schools on reading and writing. Perhaps the creation of a school Traveller pedagogy needs to emphasise this focus and find a means of educating its pupils through oral and visual modes and using their known learning styles. Teachers need to be reminded that bilingual children take longer to read and write, particularly when their mother tongue isn't taught in school. It is apparent that language is a core element of the culture of Gypsy people. The interviews suggest that Travellers' feelings about their language run deep. As Mag says, 'it's still in your blood wherever you go it's yours'.

The emphasis placed on the relative secrecy of the language may be a constraint in the development of muticultural education. There was reluctance on the part of the older Travellers to share the language. Mag's explanation was that because they had the 'language longer they treasured it'. She felt that, given the opportunity, she would have enjoyed using the language in her written work and would like to have seen reading materials that used some Romani. She said, 'I'd like to have seen it. Yes, something that we've done, something from our culture, showing we've achieved something'. The experience of schooling had made her more open to the suggestion that using Romani could be of value.

The investigation also included interviews with two reception class teachers and one headteacher. One of the reception teachers taught in a provincial school with a small intake of Traveller children, whereas the other reception teacher and the headteacher worked in an inner city school with a high intake of Gypsy children.

Because of time constraints only three teaching professionals with contrasting intakes of Gypsy children were chosen for interview. Interviewing reception teachers is important because initial school experience is so vital to the success of future schooling. The following evidence outlines some of the dilemmas facing mainstream teachers. When the teachers were asked about their awareness of home language of Gypsy children, they responded as follows.

> I know very little of home language, only the odd word like *Chore* (steal). (urban teacher).

> Very, very little, apart from the words the children have come out with.

> The only one they've mentioned is the word for Police which I've forgotten' (provincial teacher).

> I don't know a great deal. I know Romani still exists. I should know if the children speak Romani in school but honestly I don't know. It is apparent that it may help teachers if they are made aware of those words Traveller

children may use in school, which have important communicative quality irrespective of whether we consider drawing on the language in the wider pedagogy (headteacher).

The teacher from the inner city school referred to an incident in school where some Gypsy children were being called Gypsies. The Gypsy children responded by calling the offenders *gorjas*. When asked if the other children found the word *gorja* offensive, the teacher explained that the non-Gypsy children did not understand this word, 'they knew it was something unpleasant and it made them feel uncomfortable'.

She explained the children were rebuked for this name calling. Racist name calling may be seen on a continuum of from hot to cold. Cold name calling is deliberate repeated harassment in order to assert dominance whereas hot is used during heated arguments The hot situation can be divided into two instances:

• where the child regrets their actions having an understanding that it can be hurtful and then hold egalitarian beliefs.

• where the child feels the action was legitimate by way of self-defence (Troyna, 1993).

In this instance the retort *gorja* was probably hot and used in self-defence against the term Gypsy. The teacher explained that *gorja* was not brandished around so much now. The word means simply non-gypsy. It does not have the same power as the taunt of Gypsy delivered by members of the dominant culture. The other teacher from the provincial school reported that they had Gypsy children in the school for five years and no children from other ethnic minorities. Traveller culture was not reflected in any sense in the curriculum or classroom. She would possibly adapt her request for a child to draw a house to the inclusion of a trailer for the Traveller children. She pointed out that she'd never been to any Traveller children's homes and did not really know where or how they lived. However, she would adapt class talk in the same way for example by asking: 'did you hear the rain on your trailer?' She had borrowed resources from the TESS such as jigsaws of trailers.

The inner city reception teacher was more aware of Traveller culture because she had a high percentage of Traveller children and many children from other ethnic minorities. She valued their background: 'the Traveller children have a culture which they bring with them into the classroom. The school values each individual child and accepts them as who they are in their own right. The right to be wanted, the right to be in education, the classroom teacher must accommodate these rights'.

Her classroom contained an array of articles reflecting multicultural society, including those supplied by the TESS such as jigsaws, model horses and caravans, stories and photographs. When the children developed a home project, great attention was focused on the trailers modelled by the Traveller children so the class could find out more about the Traveller children's way of life. Many of the children wanted to make a trailer rather than a house. The annual visit to Appleby Horse Fair was used to encourage Traveller children to talk about their experiences. The children were given time in class to talk about their visit, how trading was done, and the types of skills in evidence. The whole class could be made more aware of the lifestyle and appreciate why, at times, some Traveller children would be absent from school.

The headteacher added that in addition to Traveller children they had Russian, Panamanian, Malaysian, Korean, Northern Chinese (Mandarin speaking), and Chinese (Cantonese speaking), amounting to 15 per cent of the school population. Resources from the TESS had been used last year for a display in the hall and the headteacher noted that the greatest interest in these resources was shown by second generation housed Travellers. Such a display celebrating cultural diversity aimed more specifically at the identifiable Traveller families in school had added value for their housed relatives.

The provincial teacher said that children were encouraged to speak and broaden their vocabulary but that home language was not drawn on. She thought that it was difficult at such a young age to draw on the home language of the children and there was also the fact that she might not recognise it. However, if a child specifically requested that they wanted to use home language for their story or news writing, she would try to help them. On the question of fostering home language in school, she thought that because there were so few Traveller children in school it would not be of great benefit for them to use it. What worried her was that she did not want to create a gap between the groups of children. She did not want to make certain children appear different, as she believed that none of the children or their parents knew there were Traveller children in school. She held the view that the children were not old enough to be prejudiced: 'the children just don't care. It would be the same if there was a green alien in the classroom, all they would be bothered about was that you're not sharing my game!'

When asked whether she thought it would be useful to have more knowledge of the Traveller children's culture, she replied that she felt it would, as 'then they know where they're coming from'. About using story books like *Shaun's Wellies*, which reflected Traveller culture but with the added content of Romani, she thought that despite her worries about causing a split, working with a whole class with this type of resource might be useful. She added 'they might like this. It would be working with something interesting and new'.

The inner city teacher told us that children would be encouraged to use home language in their story and news writing. They might draw a picture of their home (trailer) and some have asked to use the word 'shifting' – they themselves may be moving elsewhere or another family may have 'moved on'. This language diversity, whilst not Romani or Gammon, would be encouraged. She felt their language was part of their heritage and had meaning for them.

As far as it was appropriate, she would encourage the use of home language particularly in the oral news session before written work. She thought the use of home language helped the children's learning and they might feel more comfortable using it. It might enhance their self-esteem. If a child was made to use a word which made them feel uncomfortable, rather than their own particular code, it would be like the teacher saying that she didn't value the way things were said, thus subtly and indirectly undermining their heritage and culture. However, she considered it important to learn 'school language' because it opened the doors of opportunity to marginalised groups like Travellers. It was becoming more difficult for the Travellers to keep their heritage intact. In a nearby school a Travelling mother had withdrawn her children because 'they're forgetting how to be Travellers'.

On the question of language deprivation the inner city teacher described how some Traveller children were extremely articulate. By way of example, a Traveller boy had related in great detail how he had 'caught a rabbit, skinned it and put it in the pot. You could smell the rabbit cooking on the fire from the way he described it'.

The headteacher believed his teachers wouldn't draw on home language in a formal way. When children started school, teachers were encouraging freedom of expression. The children needed to know that their home backgrounds were valued, particularly when they were young. He thought publications that included home language would help.

> They would celebrate the wider diversity that exists. It is this diversity which enriches. Travellers probably do not realise the richness they can add to the school situation. Other ethnic minorities were more noticeable in this way, and, therefore, perhaps because of a weakness on our part, we don't access the aspects of language from a Traveller child that we would notice or expect from a Chinese child.

The comparison between a school with a small population of Traveller children (the provincial school) and one with a larger population of Traveller children (the inner city school) highlights the marked difference in ethos between the schools and the way they structure and organise their pedagogy.

In the former, the Travellers are afforded an incognito status with a reticence to adapt their pedagogy on the grounds that revealing their ethnicity might have negative consequences. The view held by the provincial school teacher was that children and parents were unaware of the Traveller children's ethnicity. She thought that the children were so young that prejudice was not an issue for them. The suggestions that home language could be used in story time and reading materials was met with the proviso that though it may be of use, the teacher did not want to highlight difference and thereby create divergence.

The inner city school could consider the use of home language without this worry because the Traveller children's ethnicity is openly acknowledged. The Ofsted Report advised:

> The response of school to Travelling pupils is crucially influenced by the Travelling Children's awareness of the level of their acceptance by

teachers and other pupils. Where the presence of Travelling children is openly acknowledged, and where accurate and positive images of the different nomadic communities are featured within both the resources of the school and the curriculum, then the response is lively and there is genuine openness to learning.

In contrast, where the ethos of the school implicitly or explicitly suggests that Travelling pupils are best served by an incognito status, and this is particularly so for Gypsies and New Travellers, the response lacks confidence, is tentative and reserved. This situation can also lead to behaviour difficulties.

Travelling pupils appear to achieve higher standards in schools which place great emphasis on equality of opportunity and by encouraging the acceptance of cultural and ethnic diversity, establish an ethos which fosters self-esteem and pride in individual and group identity (Ofsted, 1996).

The inner city teacher used the annual visit to Appleby Horse Fair as a pedagogical tool. The whole class was involved in a discussion before the Traveller child had the opportunity to feature the experience in their story and news writing. The school made a visit to a museum, where all the children participated in the craft skills of Gypsies. The teacher felt the Traveller children involved 'really shone'. They were proud of sharing their skills and consequently 'came into their own in the classroom'. They were able to demonstrate skills other children didn't have and assisted their peers in trying them out. Their self-esteem visibly improved according to their teacher. The visit was intended to raise the status of their cultural history and practices and negate any possible racist attitudes. The visit was organised as part of the local response to the European Year Against Racism. On the day of the visit the police were called to attend to the removal of a Gypsy trailer. According to a complainant, it had set up home in the museum grounds. In fact a Travelling family had kindly provided their Roma trailer for the children to look around and compare with the traditional Tommy Wright *Vardo* (covered wagon) housed in the museum. To add to the irony the local council who had been involved in setting up the museum project instigated calling the police. Even the local newspaper got it wrong: it described the initiative as being against antiracism!

All the teachers interviewed expressed the view that fostering home language could be useful in the curriculum and classroom. They recognised that home language was important for purposes of communication, had significance for the child, celebrated diversity, enriched the classroom and promoted self-esteem. They saw language as a vital element of the educational response to cultural diversity. It was a symbol of group identity, as was skin colour, dress or food. It was also the cause of individual and group separation when languages were not shared. It could be perceived both as a source of enrichment and as an obstacle to communication between groups.

Little research or consideration by recent policy makers in the UK has focused on the issue of the language of Travelling people. A prerequisite for the use of home language in school must be an ethos that welcomes cultural diversity openly, confidently and with competence. For those schools whose ethos presents difficulties in this respect, language may be a starting point through which they can develop a positive approach to cultural diversity. Schools should be aware that some Traveller parents may be protective of the home language and its use in school. Yet the confidence of Traveller parents must be developed. Showing an interest in their culture and encouraging work with culture specific content could increase their involvement in the school and in the curriculum.

It is recommended that the TESS can assist in promoting the use of home language in school by:

- raising awareness of commonly used words which may arise in the classroom situation

- challenging views that Traveller children are deficient in language skills

- advising teachers on naturalistic use of home language in oral and pre-writing sessions which look for similar or different words and linguistic work, exploring language connections, particularly with other minority languages

- providing reading materials which support home languages

- enabling children to feel more confident in their use of home language in school

- issuing guidelines and offering inset training on languages used by the Traveller communities

- evaluating pedagogy through AR processes

- using collaborative AR to unravel the problems of situational constraints in school ethos, ethnic composition, parental reluctance and so forth.

Since interviewing the teachers at the chosen schools there is evidence that language will be given more attention in the future. Some Travellers welcomed the value of teachers' language awareness for the pastoral care of children in the early years. A TESS coordinator has agreed to include language as an area for future consideration, following this research. John was asked to give a presentation for all TESS staff on the work outlined above.

But despite all the advantages of liberal ideological approaches, the monocultural model would appear to be the one preferred by the majority of Gypsies interviewed. They were fearful of revealing their children's ethnicity in school. They may have been internalising their oppression to escape the cycle of their own marginalisation by society. Protecting themselves meant hiding who they were and the reactions which this evoked.

Yet as the population of Traveller children attending schools grows, incognito status will be difficult to maintain. Recognition of the long standing alienation of Travelling people from the majority and its persistence today was encapsulated by the grandmother's views that 'We have been set aside for so long that we like to keep it that way.' But this kind of alienation from schooling need not continue Alienation is not a tradition, like culture, which needs to be maintained. It is an exclusive regime which should be eradicated in a culturally pluralist society. Education offers an opportunity to break the cycle of alienation and oppression which has continued into the twenty first century. From the time of their arrival in the fourteenth and fifteenth centuries Gypsies have been considered to be intruders (Liegeois, 1998). Education must directly tackle the wider social and political realities of racism through its school systems.

There is debate about what constitutes appropriate responses to cultural diversity. One answer is to create a process of evolving the pedagogy according to demand. The dichotomy between the approaches of monoculturalism and multiculturalism (or its related ideologies) includes language as an issue in the schooling of Traveller children. When reflecting on the teachers' responses we need to question the dynamics of a school that is fearful of revealing a child's ethnicity. The class teacher interviewed thought that the school situation was such that inclusion of Traveller children was best served by not divulging their ethnicity. The Travelling community has for centuries been subject to exclusion from wider society. For many Gypsies, school is an alien institution, and a threatening one. Schools which prefer to maintain incognito status for their pupils because they do not want a child to appear different from the majority are fearful about ostracism. Their attempt to protect children from the curiosity of their peers may appear commendable but it is misguided.

Monoculturalism developed in the 1960s and its ideology was based on assimilation. It centred on the suppression and reduction of ethnic, linguistic and cultural differences. A component of monoculturalism, known as the contact hypothesis, held that everyday interaction between children from ethnic minority and majority backgrounds would reduce racial prejudice and discrimination and contribute to the development of a harmonious multiracial society. Under this educational regime, the distinctive values, traditions and histories of ethnic minority pupils were at best ignored or at worst suppressed. By the late 1960s faith in this ideology began to wane yet the evidence collected in the present investigation suggests it is still very much alive in some schools. School can play a part in eliminating minority practices and culture. It can easily and effectively assimilate minority groups in its practices and even teach conformance to mainstream practices and values which are antithetical to minority cultures.

Alternative ideologies have developed whereby inclusion is pursued in support of cultural diversity. A multicultural approach seeks to reduce external prejudice by encouraging knowledge and respect of minority cultures and languages, so increasing mutual understanding. Learning is enhanced by fashioning a learning environment which embraces the value of cultural and linguistic diversity and enhances children's self-esteem. When a child's own experience, language and abilities are respected and validated, and their experience is drawn on in school, conditions for learning are optimal. Awareness is growing of the importance of maintaining community languages and according them recognition in school. Assimilationist approaches have slowly been replaced by arguments that ethnic minority children should be encouraged to maintain and develop their own linguistic and cultural resources within the school. Community languages such as Gujarati and Punjabi have higher status than Romani, although both languages bear a close relationship to Romani. Examining the links between these languages could be used as the basis of interactive exploration of multilingualism in school. If the numbers of Gypsy children in school continues to grow their presence will increase the demand for the school usage of Romani. Recognising the language of Travelling people contributes to the quality of their education.

The teachers interviewed didn't indicate any limitations in the English vocabulary of Traveller children. On the contrary, the example given of the child who described how a rabbit would be made ready for the pot illustrates expressive oral skills.

4. Early years education of Traveller children

This case story illustrates some of the challenges faced by early years Traveller educators. The early years education of Traveller children has recently been prioritised in line with government policy and initiatives. Traveller families, like any family interested in nursery school and playgroup placements for the under fives, face many practical problems regarding access, timing, transport and care of younger children. Traditionally the under fives have been kept at home because it is the place for Traveller families to manage their children and to ensure their health, safety and early learning. However, the extension of early years education provision to Travellers is imperative to provide equal educational opportunities for early growth and development in line with recent National Curriculum and standards for under fives.

Debbie was appointed as a half time teacher with responsibility for early years on a local authority project. Her main responsibility outlined in the job description were to establish the number and needs of early years Traveller pupils, to develop a working relationship with the Community Playbus Association (CPA) and other early years providers and to support the raising of achievement of Traveller pupils through the development and effective use of appropriate project resources. The practical tasks were:

- to meet with the CPA and other early years providers in order to establish and evaluate appropriate provision for Traveller pupils
- to advise project managers on resourcing strategies
- to teach young Traveller children
- to enable early years providers to increase the achievement of Traveller pupils by practical resourcing strategies
- to support early years providers in the development of their work in visiting, communicating and involving parents of Traveller pupils

These strategies were aimed at raising the early achievement of Traveller pupils. The involvement, visiting and development of relationships with parents was seen to be the most vital aspect of the plan. Providers needed to work in a partnership with families so that both children and adults would feel positively welcomed into the education system and supported in their learning.

Traditionally Traveller pre-school children have not used early years provision. The Ofsted report (1996) states that the average participation rate for Traveller children in nursery, playgroup or any other early years setting is 20 per cent. Its 1999 report shows that Gypsy Traveller pupils are the most at risk in the education system and that few of them receive any pre-school education (Ofsted 1999). Consequently many Traveller pupils enter statutory schooling with an educational disadvantage because they haven't had the benefits of early education.

Some of the reasons seen as obstacles for Travellers to participate in early years provision include:

- highly mobile Traveller families being unable to predict arrival, length of stay or departure

- parents who have not had any pre-school experience themselves, and do not place any priority or significance on early years education

- the location of sites which are often inaccessible to public transport and therefore lack of transport leads to non attendance

- Traveller parents generally are highly protective of their children and many consider children of 3-4 years too young to leave the home environment.

Family groups who had experienced hostility and marginalisation throughout their lives often make a virtue of internal mutual support and won't let young children go out of the security of the family easily (Kiddle, 1999). Also, many parents are unwilling to introduce children to pre-school activities because of their reluctance to trust strangers with their children's care.

The LEA's commitment

As early as 1992-93 the Traveller Education Project (TEP) in the LEA was aware of the need to develop its early years work. The improvement of pre-school access was stated as a project objective. Most work in this area has taken place working closely with the mobile provision provided by the local CPA.

In 1992-93 the DfE in its Annual Report proforma requested the number of Traveller children in 0-5 age group and the numbers attending under fives provision. Below are the figures provided by the LEA reflecting the low level of pre-school use by Traveller families.

Table I Numbers of pre-school children in educational contexts

	92-93	93-94	94-94	94-95	96-97	97-98
Children identified	253	83	72	93	81	81
Children in provision	35	55	35	30	38	28

However, in subsequent years the project had a cut in funding. This caused the TEP to concentrate its resources on work with statutory age children. This obviously meant that the initial work begun with the early years was no longer continued at the same level. Subsequently the TEP began to identify areas of work where improvements could be achieved.

A project SWOT analysis (Strengths, Weaknesses, Opportunities and Threats) clearly identified a lack of under fives provision as a project weakness. Interagency working was identified as a project strength. This strength proved important during the coming months as the project's bid for early years funding took shape.

Later that year the authority received details of the new Standards Fund funding for the TEP. It included a development fund aimed to finance work related to priorities which the department had identified for Traveller education in particular, improving access to pre school provision. On this basis, allied to the high needs levels for early years Traveller children in the county, targets were set to improve take-up of early years provision. The strategy to underpin this work and to achieve these targets, relied upon the appointment of a specialist responsibility post and the re-establishment of links with the CPA. The TEP's new thrust for improved early years provision for Traveller children aimed to increase the percentage of under fives provision by 2 per cent in the next year and by 4 per cent in the following two to three years. The main aim was to encourage an effective partnership between parents and practitioners in early years settings so that children felt secure, valued and confident and developed a sense of well-being and achievement.

The LEA also had a commitment to equal opportunities policy and practices: to promote equality of access and opportunity for all children irrespective of gender, ethnicity, religion, disability, culture, language or background. It promised that all sections of the community could access provision by targeted support. It recognised the importance of making provision for children whose education had been disrupted and who had limited opportunities for play. These policy statements had significant relevance for Travellers. So the research was to investigate the reality of the aims and the possibilities for their implementation and practice.

What insights could be gained into understanding Traveller values about why there was such a disparity between early education opportunities offered by LEAs and what was taken up by Traveller families? The action research itself aimed to engage the teachers, parents and children in a process of change and to make a difference in the field of early years Traveller education.

At the first LEA meeting with the co-ordinator of Traveller Education, an Early Years Action Plan was developed. The action plan emphasised the importance of networking with experienced parties which would involve the Early Childhood Unit, the CPA, Traveller Education Welfare Officers (TEWOs), Early Years Traveller Inter-Agency Group (EYTIAG), other TESS, early years providers, under eights officers, Central Minority Ethnic Curriculum Support Service (CMECSS), and health visitors. Debbie needed to obtain as much information as possible as quickly as possible. This information would be gathered by telephone to professionals concerned and through visits to Traveller families.

The number of pre-school children on county council sites and private sites had to be investigated to ascertain the numbers of under fives places needed at nursery schools, playgroups and other options in relation to a specific geographical area. This information was gleaned through visits, letters and telephone.

The most important aspect of the research was the contact with the parents of Traveller children. At first questionnaires were planned to go to parents, but that was impractical. It was difficult to find a means of communication that would be appropriate. The low up-take of pre-school provision indicated that most Traveller parents didn't come across information that was aimed at parents of young children. Among many Traveller families there was a low level of literacy. A questionnaire would be seen by many as threatening and non-productive. Face to face contact was necessary. Housed Travellers, Showmen's families and highly mobile Travellers were excluded from the research though sometime in the future this will be reviewed. The interviews were semi-structured, asking certain pre-set questions but allowing interviewees freedom to digress and raise their own topics as the interview progressed. They were planned to be flexible to allow other topics to be raised, to encourage parents to talk in the context of the early years. The interviews were to be used in building rapport to establish relationships.

A simple interview schedule was devised after some discussion about piloting the questions with colleagues. The purpose of using a tape recorder was explained and parents' permission was requested for its use. However, the first interview taped was unsuccessful. The tape recorder was large and after asking permission it was placed on the floor of the trailer. When a three year old boy came in and saw the machine it was hard to persuade him to leave it alone. When the tape was played back it was clear that Debbie had done much of the talking and it didn't give a clear picture of what the issues were. It was decided to take a notebook to future interviews and to record parental responses. Consideration was given to factors that commonly arise in interviewing such as, eagerness to please the interviewer, a vague antagonism that sometimes arises between interviewer and respondent, the tendency of the interviewer to seek out the answers that support preconceived notions. After the first few interviews the questions came naturally to Debbie who interviewed 53 parents, all except two of them mothers.

Debbie also kept a journal recording her reflections and progress during the investigation. Looking back at her journal entries after the completion of the research she was surprised how ignorant and yet concerned she felt at the beginning.

Debbie's line manager took her to a site for her first interview. She had known the families well for many years and been on community consultations with them. She introduced Debbie to the matriarch of the site and her daughter-in-law who had a two year old boy. She wrote about the mother, 'she was very open to the thought of nursery and hopes he will go. He will not go if he is unhappy about it.'

There were ten county council sites and the task was to interview all the parents of children under five living on them and on two private sites. Locating the sites proved extremely time consuming, because the map was not accurate and some of the sites had disappeared. The TEWO and Gypsy section of the LEA were also unaware of their whereabouts.

The health visitors attached to each site were contacted and were asked to accompany Debbie to the sites. The first site was almost empty. It was a relatively new site and many of the families travelled in the summer months. The mother interviewed was a parent Debbie had known for four years because she had supported her older children at primary and secondary school. She had a four year old son.

She was very worried about nursery and during the interview her youngest child lay on the bunk watching a video, sucking a bottle, stroking his comfort pillow. An appointment was made to go and see her in three weeks as she was shifting off and travelling the next day. However she didn't come back to the site until the end of the summer holidays when she was taken with her son Sonny to visit the local nursery class. Sonny had a wonderful time there and especially liked the work bench. His mother put his name down, agreed that he should go on school trips and seemed happy about the security arrangements. But he has only attended once since then.

Another site visit with a health visitor revealed that she was not happy to be visiting the site with Debbie. Yet with the help of the site warden she was reassured. Wardens on the county council sites are in a difficult position as their job entails not only supporting the families to maintain the plot, but also having to enforce unpopular rules and collect rent arrears. Sometimes relationships between wardens and Travellers become strained. However, the introductions that the warden and health visitor gave Debbie were valuable, and on that site she was able to interview four parents.

Interviewees can feel threatened and this aspect of collecting data can be influenced by the relationships established between the participants. Parents who had encountered difficulties with the education system in their youth felt intimidated by an interview, but the health visitor and the warden helped create a positive initial meeting. Difficulty in accessing the parents was a persistent problem in the research.

Eighty per cent of the parents interviewed said they knew nothing about pre-school education, but most of them agreed that children needed to learn certain things before they went to school. One young woman, on an isolated site with a five month old baby, said 'Travellers won't be able to fell trees much longer. They need education.' Other parents mentioned the need to socialise and mix with non-Travellers. One parent on the site said that she felt that nursery 'breaks them in for big school'.

Five parents admitted being reluctant to send their children to pre-school provision. Four had nursery places. In each case it was a youngest son and there was a fear of allowing them to attend the provision because: 'He won't like it, he wants to stay at home with me, he can escape from anywhere and I can't trust a nursery to stop him running away'. When one of the parents visited the nursery where her son had a place, she said that he could get out of the out-door playing area even though it had a high locked gate. All five parents had older children attending school yet because the younger son was their latest baby, they wanted to keep him as long as possible in the home environment.

Another local site which was settled and established, where Travel-lers didn't travel at any time of the year, had thirty big plots with gardens and three parents had their children in the local nursery and two had their children's names down for the same nursery. One mother of a two year old was extremely anxious to get her son into playgroup. She said he loved being left in the crèche at Asda.

When Debbie was interviewing parents a number of them requested that she accompany them on visits to local playgroups and find places for their children. Of the four parents who had places at play-group only one was attending regularly. There were different reasons for this. One parent thought her child was too young, one had com-plications with her older children not attending school and one had transport problems. The parents needed constant encouragement to use the LEA provision.

All the county council sites, except one, were inaccessible to shops and schools. They were set in the middle of the countryside, often behind high grassy banks and on the edge of main roads. On one of the sites there were three children who should have been attending nursery classes and couldn't go because the family had no transport. The walk to the nursery was down a disused railway line and when another smaller child had to be taken as well, in a push chair, the journey became impossible.

Discussions had been held at the TEP meetings about transport issues. The Early Childhood Unit had some money in the partner-ship's Early Childhood Initiative Fund available for transport, if it could be costed up and a formal bid made for this money. Providing transport would be an interim measure to cut down the constraints for Travellers in early years provision.

The playbus

Almost all the Traveller parents said that they wanted on-site provision because of their anxiety about the safety of their children. The playbus which was being used on three sites was a converted double decker bus that was designed and equipped to offer early learning experiences to young children. The provision operated for isolated communities in a large county, but other choices could have been made. The bus was used as an immediate means of making progress. It was used specifically for families who were isolated or lacked access to facilities. On all three sites the children clearly benefited from attending the playbus. Also on one of the sites the children were attending the local playgroup as a result of going on the bus. It was decided to hire a van equipped with resources and a part-time worker from the CPA. It was a custom built van donated by Save the Children, with work surfaces on one side, an elevated section accessed by a ladder and room for a sand-pit and other equipment. It was to be taken to another site once a week.

The TEP devised clear cut aims for the playvan as follows:

- to provide early years experience to Travellers

- develop working relationships with the staff of CPA

- assess use and suitability of early years resources

- foster independence of children and trust in early years providers.

The provision aimed to bridge the gap between no early years provision and mainstream nursery provision through information sharing, relationship building and escorted visits to mainstream provision.

Existing resources were used in the playvan and more equipment was provided as necessary. The CPA worker and Debbie went to the selected site once a week and it proved highly effective. There were at least five children on the van every week and they did activities it would have been difficult to do in the trailer, such as painting, building, climbing, gluing, modelling, and sand play. The van was parked on an empty plot so it was safe to have outside activities as a nearby gate could be shut. Parents were encouraged to stay, but usually the children were left in the van for the duration of the site session. Trust was established with the parents and two of the children were enrolled in a local playgroup and, though not regulars, they did attend from time to time. Another child started the nursery of the school where she was enrolled in the reception class. The playvan acted as a bridge to mainstream provision. It was planned to take the van to two more sites. On one site a mother had volunteered her plot for the playvan to allow the children to engage in outside activities. The playvan was subsequently recognised an example of good practice.

Play boxes

Almost all the parents said they believed that children needed to learn something before they went to school. In order to help parents achieve this play boxes were created, early learning boxes and baby play boxes, all of which had activities which were based on the government's early learning goals. The boxes were designed as an encouragement to parents, as an example of first hand play opportunities and not as an alternative to out of nursery or school provision. They were to give parents the skills to develop meaningful play with their children and to give them their first experience of the expectations of the government's early learning goals which form baseline assessment. Overall the boxes ensured that children entering playgroup or nursery had the experiences that would enable them to participate fully in school based activities.

Playbox aims, guidelines for their use and a photographic booklet for parents with low literacy skills were produced. The activities for each box were created to reflect each early learning goal: creative development, physical development, language and literacy, mathematics, knowledge of the world and personal development. The items were high quality and easily maintained. Parents who received the boxes were shown, with their child, how to use each activity in the box, to ensure that all the activities would be done in the home after the early years worker left. The play boxes were to be changed regularly and as appropriate for each child's needs. The venture is to be evaluated for wider dissemination.

When looking back, Debbie can see how much has changed as a result of her interventions in the provision of early years in the LEA. Her investigation has changed attitudes, responses, attendance, awareness and the processes instigated as a result of the research. The building of relationships to change Traveller parents' perceptions about the educational needs of their young children is proving to be a slow process. When the figures for nursery and playgroup attendance include children who attend the playvan and playbus, the numbers show a healthy rise, and together they add up to the LEA target of more than 2%. Children who attended regularly showed improved concentration and their painting and play dough work also showed creative development. Most of the children were able to sit and listen to a story after settling in. The workers on the playbus said that the Traveller aspect of their work was the most fulfilling they did because the response and development of the children was so dramatic.

Debbie's practitioner research has helped her to achieve her professional job targets. It was a successful means of discovering what the Traveller parents and children actually wanted and needed and it formed a basis for renewed practice in the LEA's early years provision.

5. Developing literacy

The following case story examines the development of literacy with Traveller pupils. Lou has recently taken up the post of literacy co-ordinator for Traveller pupils in the LEA. She attended a meeting at the three main schools she was working in. Colleagues were very happy to listen and offer their opinions, but at the same time they made it clear that systems were established in their schools and that they were not ready to adapt. She would be made very welcome in their schools as long as she did not expect anything from them. They seemed to be saying 'take the raw materials, the kids, and bring us back some children who will fit more easily into the systems that we have in place. And leave us the answers so we can change any other Travellers we may have in school.'

She felt that this was a job that she was going to have to do on her own. She didn't want the Travellers to disappear; she wanted to support their success. She thought that what was common practice for many other cultures in schools was still a rarity for Travellers.

She carried out her investigation in three schools.

School A was an inner city primary school in a predominantly Asian area. A three form entry school, it had eleven children from four Traveller families on roll.

School B was an inner city Roman Catholic primary school, also in a predominantly Asian area, but with a higher proportion of white children. It was a favourite with Travellers because of its church connections, and the opportunity was offered to learn prayers and to prepare for Holy Communion. It had a one and a half form entry with eight Traveller children from three families on roll.

School C was an inner city primary school in a very ethnically diverse area, which was the closest school to the authority's only permanent site. It had a one and a half form entry with twenty Traveller children from eleven families.

All three schools had a history of educating Traveller children. Procedures, therefore, would be in place and staff would have experience of working with Traveller children. Professional development and INSET training had also been given. Each of the schools had a named link person, known as the Traveller liaison teacher, who acted as a point of contact for the Traveller children and their parents, school staff and the TESS.

The next step was to identify the children with whom the intensive programmes would run initially. Criteria were drawn up for children at Key Stage 2 where it was felt that the difference in school attainment between Traveller pupils and their settled peers was most marked. This also allowed children time for delayed natural development in the early years, especially if they had missed out on a nursery education and had none of the expected parental support, pre school, in the early stages of literacy acquisition. Ten children were identified and were chosen for their literacy needs as well as other socially related reasons.

School A

Bill was a Year 6 boy who was displaying demanding behaviour. He was under threat of exclusion from the school, as teachers were finding him very difficult to manage. It was recognised by all concerned that much of his inappropriate behaviour was a diversionary tactic, so he could divert attention away from his poor literacy skills. It was hoped that a literacy programme that would improve his basic skills would have a positive affect on his behaviour.

Bruce was a year 4 boy whose parents had a close relationship with members of the TESS. They were very concerned that their children should leave school literate and this they described as a favour to them.

Angie was a year 7 girl the school had agreed to keep for an extra year, due to her extreme nervousness. Her attendance was quite poor and it was hoped that, with additional support and attention, this would improve. She had a low level of literacy, and it was considered necessary to address this before she left the school, as it was a concern that she might not transfer to secondary school.

Mark was in year 6 and was included as a substitute for Angie in case her poor attendance ruled her out. He was due to receive a statement of special educational needs. He was not included in the initial identification as it was felt that his needs were due to learning difficulties rather than gaps in learning.

School B
In the second school three girls with literacy difficulties were identified, one in Year 6 and two in Year 3. They were all reasonably regular attenders, who had been on roll for some time. They were not considered to have special educational needs, yet were not making equivalent progress to that of their peers. They were: Barbara from Year 6, Melanie from year 4, and Debra from year 4.

School C
Julie was identified, as it was felt that with some intervention she would make noticeable progress. She was in year 4.

John was identified as it was felt that the programme would help ascertain whether his needs were due to his mobility and having missed so much school, or whether he had special educational needs that would be better addressed through statementing via the code of practice. John was also in Year 4.

Maggie was identified mainly for political reasons. Her father was the 'main man' on the Traveller site. Relationships between her father and team members had broken down and it was acknowledged that his influence could work for or against the education of the Traveller children. A stated anxiety of his was that he had sent all his children to school regularly but they still couldn't read. It was felt that if he knew Maggie was working with a special reading teacher it might start to build bridges. It would also give Lou a platform to visit the family and tell them what was happening, and re-establish contact between the residents of the site and the TESS.

Assessments of the children took the form of a concepts of print test adapted from Marie Clay, a letter recognition assessment of both graphemes and phonemes, and a reading and spelling assessment related to the appendices in the National Literacy Strategy which included a record of miscues. A profile of each child was thus built up, and related to the phases in the *First Steps Developmental Continuum* (Rigby, 1998) which provide very small steps and guide the teacher through logical stages of progression. Often the attainment of Traveller children who do not have consistent attendance cannot be demonstrated through more usual forms of assessment such as SATs or QCA tests. Therefore it can appear that no progress has been made because there is no formal means of recording the enormous leaps the children might have made. This thorough assessment also included a period of conversation with the children in order to relax them and find out additional relevant information, likes and dislikes for instance, which could inform the planning.

With this information a programme of targets was devised, using the developmental continuum as a guide. Once established, the programmes were easy to follow and demonstrated where and when progress had been made.

The children were to receive three sessions a week, two from the literacy co-ordinator and one provided by the school. The third session was to relate to the programme and address the targets identified. The advice of the TESS co-ordinator was that three sessions a week rather than two were required of the literacy co-ordinator if progress was to be made.

The second part of the research focused on helping Traveller children to increase their access to the literacy hour. After initial observations Lou assisted with planning and preparation for the shared reading and writing sessions, as well as preparing activities for the group work time. She shared the delivery of the whole class sessions and sometimes led the literacy hour so the class teachers could make observations of their own.

The introduction of the National Literacy Strategy (NLS) claimed to provide a consistent approach to the teaching of reading and writing nationally. It advocated a method of teaching where skills were made explicit, where differentiation was paramount, where children were working towards the same ends, though taking different paths to get there. Through the shared reading and writing sessions that were an integral part of the hour, Traveller children would have access to interesting and stimulating text, an opportunity to draw them into the world of literature, rather than abandoning them on one specific reading scheme for ever. For Traveller support teachers it appeared to provide the answer but, as with any strategy, there was no guarantee of how it would be delivered. Instead of being a tool for inclusion it was often being used as a tool to justify exclusion, and many Traveller children were being differentiated out of the sessions that would have benefited them most.

At the end of her first half term in post Lou was able to track and provide evidence that the targeted children had made some progress. What was difficult to assess was what this meant in the broader picture. Each child had an increased sight vocabulary, knew more letters and phonemes and had demonstrated increased skills on the developmental continuum. What she couldn't assess was whether this had made any long term difference to their literacy levels. The evidence of this would be in their ability to use the strategies shown in the sessions independently, to inform their reading and writing. If there was an improvement, how could it be known whether it was due to the literacy co-ordinator, the class teacher, or the child's natural development?

Lou realised from keeping a professional journal throughout that she needed to adapt her work in several ways. She needed long term objectives that were to be broken down into weekly targets, in order to focus on each child's achievements. These targets needed to be linked to the objectives in the NLS framework for them to be relevant to class teachers. This would also help to achieve the overall aim of reintegration and increased access to the literacy hour.

The withdrawal sessions themselves needed to be reconsidered in light of the fact that no school had taken up the offer of a co-ordinated session. This was initially made a prerequisite for support but had proved impossible to administer in practice because time for individual school visits was difficult when visiting numerous schools, and they were reluctant to take responsibility for the literacy sessions. The only way they could give additional time to the children was in groups, and then the literacy objectives were led by the class teacher and the literacy co-ordinator's objectives related to Traveller children might not be relevant to the rest of the group.

The progress the children made during the withdrawal sessions was negligible. The sessions were interrupted by periods of absence, time-tabling changes within school, the search for an appropriate work area, and discussion about children's personal issues when they found a sensitive ear. These sessions were not taken seriously by the schools. Many of the class teachers had shown no interest in the work being carried out beyond the classroom, some were simply relieved to have some time when they didn't need to consider the Traveller child. The act of withdrawing them from the classroom continued to keep them separate rather than included.

The most restricting factor had been other people's perceptions of what Lou was doing. Her line manager wanted her to remain quite separate and distinct from her mainstream colleagues. He was convinced that the individual withdrawal sessions were the way forward for Travellers. The inspector for English and drama would have liked Lou to be more in line with school based literacy co-ordinators but in a position to highlight Traveller issues. Schools' established literacy co-ordinators wanted her to stay away because they felt she did not understand the issues relevant for the whole school. So she spent time explaining herself to colleagues and re-establishing her role.

Lou felt that her research, and subsequent evidence, would have had more conclusive results had she been able to base herself in one school, with a single cohort of children. She would then have been able to say to other schools 'This is what I have done at another school'. The nature of the job pressured her into being there for all of the children. Yet with frequent pupil absences, this often meant that there were huge time lapses between the sessions. With the focus on just one school at a time, spending a day there, it might have been possible to demonstrate to class teachers how Traveller culture could be integrated into the curriculum.

From the work Lou has carried out, she believes the way forward to improve Traveller education is through curriculum integration. The schools need to see their responsibilities towards these children, and plan for them appropriately in each lesson. The NLS provides an opportunity for Traveller children to develop their literacy skills and to start to see the relationship between written and spoken language. It is here that the role of the specific Traveller literacy co-ordinator needs to be developed.

It is vital that Traveller children derive full benefit from the NLS. Children travelling and attending schools across the country during the year will then receive a consistent approach to the teaching of literacy, and will meet the same content in any one term, in any one school. Pupils will always get a skills input, even if attendance is intermittent. Children will have the opportunity to raise questions following input and to draw upon their oral ability, so giving them increased opportunities to excel.

The investigation was successful in raising the profile of Traveller children within the LEA, but it needed more status and support from LEA management to initiate the changes necessary to significantly raise standards. Schools must recognise Travellers as a distinct culture and make moves to respond to them, not try to force Traveller children to fit the existing systems. In order for Lou's work to be truly effective she should be peripatetic but in a strategic way. She would like to spend a block of time in one school to have greater input into planning, including that of classes where there are no Traveller children at present. It is necessary to have a whole school approach to raising standards and to ensure that this addresses Traveller children's needs and thus improves literacy skills within the Traveller community.

6. Inclusion in schooling

Paula's case study involved her own professional practice as a Traveller advisor in an LEA. Her story is about solving an educational problem which was defined through an investigative process.

Paula's main aim was to include Traveller children and young people in schools in the local authority. She began by questioning the assumed association with SENCOs made by schools about Traveller pupils. There had been a move since the 1981 Education Act for schools to become more inclusive. However, a number of schools and LEAs tended to concentrate on children with special educational needs when referring to inclusive education. So when they made the case for Travellers' entitlement to inclusion in mainstream classrooms, many professionals wrongly assumed that Travellers had special educational needs. The point of liaison for a Traveller Education Support Service (TESS) which tries to arrange support for Traveller pupils, is often the school's Special Educational Needs Coordinator (SENCO). Although SENCOs usefully help make specific arrangements for pupils, working through them labels and stigmatises Travellers as having learning difficulties.

Travellers have a statutory right to appropriate provision, not because they have special educational needs, but because they have gaps in their schooling due to their culture and lifestyle. Traveller pupils' educational difficulties could be compared to those of children for whom English is an additional language (EAL), many of whom have experienced school in other countries. Although becoming literate in a second language is often a problem for them, they are predominantly competent in their own first language. Also, schools often have more tolerance for children who speak a different language, than they have for English first speakers who cannot read or write and who don't live in settled homes. Paula wrote,

> I have chosen to do this action research because I think that many Traveller children are not fully included in many schools. I want to find the way forward for the Traveller Service and to find out how the recipients of education, in this case the Traveller child, feels about educational practices working to improve their education to make schools an environment where all children can learn together. The action arising from the outcomes of the research will depend on the findings.

After discussion with colleagues Paula decided to use a question-naire initially to collect evidence about what was happening and this was delivered to all Traveller children in the LA. Questions were related to the academic, social and extra-curricular activities of the schools they attended. The questionnaire was also used as a prompt for questions in pupil interviews. Children were interviewed in a relaxed atmosphere, on their own territory and as far as possible without their siblings. A code of practice was read and discussed with each child before interviewing, and to inform them that other children would be answering the same questions. Parental permission was also sought for each child participating in the investigation. A journal of events and reflections about what occurred in school and on home visits was also kept. This provided another perspective to the interviews, because it included evidence from Traveller parents, teachers and colleagues. Any matters that arose in relation to schooling or education were to be included in an action research record.

Fourteen children from seven different schools were interviewed. There were six boys, eight girls, twelve primary and two secondary pupils. Three pupils were living on a Traveller site and the others in short-stay housing.

The interview questions yielded mixed results. When pupils were asked what they liked and disliked about school, the highest scores came from pupils liking school because they liked the teachers, and disliking it because of bullies. Maths lessons were the most favoured lessons whereas science lessons were most disliked. The majority of children enjoyed break-times. They played mainly with friends or relatives. One child played only with relatives. Most children walked to school or came by van or car. They generally wanted to get to school on time and didn't like being off school or coming in not knowing where they were with their school-work. All had been in concert performances or drama activities and only two had not played monitor or done jobs for the teacher. When asked what they wanted to change in schools, individual teachers were the first choice, followed equally by stopping bullying, friendlier children, and longer playtimes. One child wanted to get rid of school uniforms so it would be easier for her cousins to come to the school.

Paula had reservations about the interviews:

> The problem with asking questions like those on the questionnaire is that children often think there is a correct answer, or that you are expecting to hear a particular answer. They also tend to tell you what has happened to them that day, or particular events with special significance for them. The questions only manage to scratch the surface because many of them are embarrassed, or reluctant to admit that other children do not want to play with them, or that they have a problem with a particular teacher. They only have their own experiences to call upon and they think that the way they are treated is the norm for everyone. They cannot compare their treatment objectively with that of others. The children may not interpret their feelings as those of being excluded, or may to try to hide them when talking to an adult in a professional role.

Other events which were recorded in the journal were more helpful in providing evidence for what the Traveller children and families were experiencing. For example an educational welfare officer contacted Paula about a girl who had recently transferred to secondary school and was encountering problems with Physical Education (PE). She had refused to get changed into PE clothing for a lesson. The secondary school had contacted her recent primary school, which confirmed that she had never changed for PE in their school. Paula visited her mother, who told her she had been to the school, discussed the matter and felt that her daughter should be changing for PE and participating in the lessons. She hadn't realised she was refusing PE in primary school and wanted her to participate because it was a girls only school, so there should be no problems about changing because there were no boys. Her daughter Jan was agreeable to this. However, Jan had filled in a questionnaire about participation in school and hadn't indicated anything related to a problem of non-participation in PE. On reflection, Paula thought that it would have been better to give the questionnaire to a whole class including Traveller children, rather than just Travellers. In that way she would have been able to make more relevant comparisons, as triangulated information from a third party would have challenged and modified her assumed objectivity.

The journal was particularly useful because it provided evidence from a different perspective to the questionnaire and picked up on specific events and ideas the pupils may not have known about. It benefited the research because a triangulation of evidence from three different perspectives could be compared and contrasted.

Reviewing evidence from the journal revealed much to feel satisfied about in terms of the children feeling included. Traveller children were mixing with classmates, going on school trips, being picked by peers to join in playtime, school teams and games, participating fully in all class activities in and outside school. Many parents had attended parents' meetings but there were some incidents which caused concern. A mother telephoned because she had moved house and couldn't get her children into local schools. Paula phoned the LEA office to ask that this mother be sent a Secondary Transfer Form and also enquired about the availability of primary places. It appeared that the local school had had a fire and there was a short-age of school places. There was also a general reluctance in schools to take new pupils late in the school year with sports days and out-ings etc.

Access to schooling was still a major issue and many other Traveller families in the local area had a similar problem. Personnel in the LEA accepted there was a problem with access and promised to do what they could when specific situations arose.

A class teacher reported that because one girl's baby sister had been ill, the family had spent time visiting hospital so the girl had taken a lot of time off school because the family had no child-care support. Paula contacted the family to offer ideas for support to ensure that their daughter attended school. They were new in the area and knew few people who could possibly help out. She approached the school for ideas and they offered to try to find after-school care and pos-sible transport from other parents for the pupil.

After visiting the local Traveller site Paula heard that two families had received letters about their children's unauthorised school ab-sences. One mother couldn't understand the letter and as the dates referred to in the letter were some time ago, she was confused be-cause her son had recently been attending every day.

Paula explained to her how the school system worked for pupils who were noted absent and spoke to the school about finding a possible way to communicate with parents who didn't read or write, if their children were ill or otherwise unable to attend. The school agreed to raise the issue at the next Governors' meeting involving staff.

During a home visit a mother related that she had asked her child's headteacher to write a letter to help her family to be re-housed. The headteacher had not yet written the letter. The mother thought the reason for this was related to recent contacts with her family. Negotiation on the family's behalf reassured the Traveller family about the school's positive attitudes and motives towards their son's education.

School trips were also a problem for many Traveller families. Contingency arrangements were presented to the LEA and school staff about ways of ensuring that all Traveller pupils would participate in school trips. The Traveller pupils did successfully participate in activities during the school day, like swimming and museum trips, but weekend and after school activities needed to be strengthened between families and schools.

The evidence showed that Traveller children felt included in extra-curricular activities in primary school, whereas in secondary school they were often independent enough to be able to make their own arrangements or to apply pressure on their parents for them to take part.

Parental appointments with schools were a problem and communication was not easy because many of the Traveller parents were illiterate. Yet the school had to address these issues and find a way to communicate to avoid the children feeling excluded. The investigation found instances of bullying and children being ostracised outside the classroom, but these were diminishing.

Discussions have been held about the issues raised in the research and currently more inter-school and inter-home liaison is being created to reduce the constraints to Traveller children participating fully in school. When the school SENCO was approached about an INSET (inservice training) session, she felt that some of the staff would benefit from additional knowledge about Travellers as it might enlighten their attitudes. An INSET session for all staff on the topic of Traveller schooling has since been organised.

Paula has become more involved with staff in local schools through INSET days and through developing contributions to the school's equal opportunities policy. Traveller issues are being included in the curriculum through partnership teaching; lessons which question the use of stereotypical images and confront racism, bullying or name-calling; the use of role play, circle time, drama and PSHE lessons are all being used for challenging negative stereotypes of Travellers. The school has agreed to work in partnership with the TESS in teaching these lessons and arranging professional development days for the staff. The research has enabled the TESS to implement plans in this local authority for more inclusive practice for Traveller pupils.

Post-script

After Paula's efforts on behalf of her pupils in her LEA a radio interview was broadcast with Jack Straw, Secretary of State (Annie Oathen, Radio West Midlands 26th August 1999) in which he said:

> Now I think the first thing we have to say is that people have to stop being sentimental about so-called Travellers. There are relatively few Romany Gypsies left, who seem to mind their own business and don't cause trouble to other people, and then there are a lot more people who masquerade as Travellers or Gypsies. They trade on the sentiment of people, but seem to think because they label themselves as Travellers that therefore they've got a licence to commit crimes and act in an unlawful way that other people don't have.
>
> In the past I'm afraid there has been rather too much toleration of Travellers and we want to see Police and local authorities cracking down on them. They're living in the margins of society. Many of these so-called Travellers seem to think that it's perfectly okay for them to cause mayhem in an area, to go burgling, thieving, breaking into vehicles, causing all kinds of other trouble including defecating in the doorways of firms and so on, and getting away with it, then their behaviour deteriorates. If the West Midlands police and the local authorities are toughening up on their approach to Travellers, as I believe is entirely justified, then they'll get the message and they'll change their behaviour.

This broadcast precipated a backlash against Travellers. Head-teachers in one LEA received emails warning them about Travellers possibly invading school sites, which concluded by warning that members of school staff should not approach the Travellers.

As a result of the broadcast there appears to have been a nation wide surge of hostility towards Travellers. So now the TESS is having to make additional efforts to eradicate negative and inaccurate stereotypes, which reinforce segregation practices in education. The political macro and micro aspects of making education inclusive for Travellers combine in a very uneasy alliance.

7. Increasing the school attendance of Traveller children

The DfES, through the Ethnic Minorities and Traveller grant in the Standards Fund, actively supports the increased school attendance of Traveller children and a link is acknowledged between the attendance levels of the children and the understanding and contact with the parents. The poor communication and lack of understanding between the school and the parents and of the need to work together to ensure that students take full advantage of educational opportunities offered to them is recognised (DES, 1990).

In the LEA where Chris works there are winter bases for a large number of Showmen's families. The families begin the travelling season at the middle or end of March and return to the area for the winter in mid November. Consequently, the children leave school before Easter time and return after the half-term break, so missing between one and two terms at school. The pupils travel with distance learning work of varying quality. The families return for occasional weeks during the summer to check equipment or for local bookings. They also sometimes work within a short distance of the winter base. But despite visits home, the pupils very rarely returned to school till mid-November. Chris' work with parents aims to develop a better understanding of the education system and promote its value in order to increase school attendance. Her aim was to increase attendance at the winter base school so that:

- the percentage of authorised absences would fall
- less school work would be missed by the pupils therefore school achievement would improve
- the distance learning work could be targeted more appropriately.

The families, it was hoped, would benefit by:

- possibly fulfilling the number of attendances required by law
- improved continuity of education and increased attainment
- increased potential for completing their education and increasing future choices.

Chris needed to find out whether work done with the targeted parents had been fruitful, and how to improve on the success rate. She also needed to assess whether the outcomes warranted the input of resources from the TESS, bearing in mind that action research deliberately aims to improve the quality of the real situation (O'Hanlon, 1995).

The research was aimed at parents from a secondary and a primary school, who all lived on two sites in the area. It also included an evaluation of initiatives outlined below:

- a group of parents were involved in a course aimed at helping them understand the formal education system at a national, local and personal level. It was hoped that by understanding some of the pressures, constraints and legal requirements that influenced their child's education, they would be better prepared to understand how their child fitted into the system and how as parents they could support them.

- parents with children on roll at a local secondary school were actively encouraged to attend a meeting to discuss how to improve the educational opportunities for their children. The aim of the meeting was to discuss the open and distance learning system that the pupils, parents and children used. Parents were visited prior to the meeting to help clarify any issues and concerns they had and were supported at the meeting so that they could fully express their views.

- Parents with pre school aged children were offered support sessions for their children to aid the transition to primary school. These visits offered an opportunity for general discussion on the role of education and how it fitted into the Traveller lifestyle.

The investigation also aimed to assess whether:

- there was an increase in the attendance of the children from the families targeted

- the work done with the families had impacted on school attendance

This was done by:

- comparing attendance during the summer term for the three previous years when families were travelling some of the time

- comparing the number of teaching visits requested during the period of travel over the summer

- interviewing the parents to discuss their views after attending the course

- a questionnaire to the teachers at two primary schools: the one that had participated in the formal course input to parents and the other where parents had received informal input during pre-school sessions

- recording the issues and concerns in a journal, the relevance of the investigation focus and any personal involvement and biases. It also noted action taken and reflection.

Data collection

Statistical data for the summer term and the two previous years was collected. This data was already obtained from the schools and was easily accessible. Comparing the data would show if there had been an increase in attendance and if there had been a difference in the use of visiting teachers. The data would not however illuminate the reasons for any change that had taken place, or provide information to aid analysis of why.

Interviews with parents

The interviews ranged from structured to unstructured (Bell, 1993). The structured interview was controlled and standardised so the re-sulting information was easy to analyse, but it didn't allow for ex-pansion of opinions nor consider issues not addressed by the question – which might not be the most appropriate one. The unstructured interview allowed for an abundance of data but required great skill to control the interview and also time to analyse the information col-lected.

The interviews used a list of questions but also allowed expansion on the selected topics. Their reliability had to be considered: different answers might have resulted from the timing of the interviews and who carried them out. Chris had her personal biases, and other factors added dimensions, such as:

- the long term professional relationship she held with the parents (over six years)

- the positive experiences that had been shared with parents during the course

- opinions and expectations of the course were known by the parents (discussed during the last session of the course)

- parents knew Chris' professional role and the role of the organisation

- the parents' possible desire to give positive responses regardless of the truth.

Four parents were interviewed, two in a face to face joint interview recorded on audio tape, one in a face to face and another over the telephone, with notes taken simultaneously. Five parents could not be contacted before the end of the research period due to their extended working periods.

Questionnaires

Personal interviews with all the staff of the two schools were not possible so they answered a questionnaire. Questions were constructed to find if there had been a recent change in parents' attitudes towards their involvement in formal education. These were then piloted with colleagues and friends. Although they could not answer the questions, their views on clarity were helpful. The questionnaires were distributed to the schools, the purpose was explained and both schools agreed to help. They were collected two days later.

The staff of one school had all completed it, some choosing the option to remain anonymous. The headteacher of the other school expressed concern about completing them so near the end of term, and only one was completed.

Journal

A personal journal was kept of the research. It recorded the issues and concerns experienced, the relevance they had to the research, Chris's personal involvement in them and any biases she could honestly identify. The action taken was recorded and there were reflections on what had evolved. The journal was used to clarify issues, explore explanations and record justifications and decisions for action. It allowed Chris to reflect on the process, analyse evidence thoughts and ideas and improve the situation. O'Hanlon (1997) identifies four styles of journal writing, of which Chris aspired to deliberative writing, as it supported her reflexive writing and self-understanding about decision making.

Earlier inputs with parents aimed to informally improve parental understanding of the education system: the school's place in the national picture, their child's place in schooling and their children's rights.

There were three phases in the research:

- identification of data and information to be collected

- decisions about its method of collection

- collection of data and information from government statistics, questionnaires, and interviews.

The process began by identifying the pupils and parents who had received the input via: the accredited course, the meeting at the secondary school or the pre-school support.

The categories of relevant information and the methods used to collect them were as follows:

- questionnaires for teachers and headteachers who had parents that received the input

- questions for the secondary school, which had the meeting for parents

- collection of attendance data of the identified pupils over three years

- questions created for parents

- interviews of a selection of parents

- collection of data related to the number of teachers' visits received while travelling during three years. This was to be done by using the Monitoring Visit Report sheets returned to the TESS by the visiting teachers.

Once the tasks were identified, two lists were made: one of the families who had received input and one about the type of input received. This produced a list of six key families who had received two out of the three inputs delivered and three reserve families who had received only the informal input. Chris attended a school staff meeting where the questions could be discussed by the staff.

Problems contacting and interviewing Traveller parents

Interviewing the parents identified as the six key families was difficult. The families had been travelling since the beginning of May and the expected date of return was in October or November. It was hoped that when the parents had returned to the area they could be contacted and interviewed while they were at the home base.

In the first week in September one key family returned to the home base for two days and with them was one of the other key families. Parents from both families agreed to be interviewed and appointments were made for the next week when they would be back. Another key family reported that more work was available so they would not be returning to the home base till after Christmas. But this parent was keen to take part in the research and suggested a telephone interview.

The following week the first of the two interviews arranged took place with a parent from each key family. Because they were moving off the next day they asked to do the interview together to save time. They both agreed to a tape-recorded interview. The interview went well and lasted just over one hour, including general discussion about the season, the whereabouts of other families and issues around the distance learning work. Not all of this was taped.

The following week a visit to a key family was arranged for an interview. The parent seemed a little uneasy and declined to have the interview taped. She was offered the option of not proceeding but she said that the interview should go ahead. The parents' younger children were present during the interview.

The two remaining key families could not be contacted and a family relative reported that they would not be back till the end of November. The site warden said that the three families from another site identified as possible reserve families had given up their pitches and would not be returning. Due to the time restrictions it was decided to end this aspect of the investigation at the end of October.

Review of data/information.

The attendance figures showed a marked increase – from three to five times the number of attendances in previous years for all pupils. There was an increase from 0 to 20 attendances for two pupils whose parents received only one input. Only two primary and secondary pupils did not attend more often.

Monitoring visits showed that the number of pupil visits from a visiting teacher during the summer remained similar to the previous two years. But although the results do indicate some success in the interventions, extraneous factors which may be relevant are not taken into account, such as that change in work patterns that kept the families closer to the home base, and that the number of teacher visits increased. Moreover, family contacts with school had dramatically increased and facilitated extra attendances.

Overall, the investigation showed how any planned research is limited by unforeseen factors. Some were endemic to the situation, like the constant and irregular movement of Traveller families. Others are integral to any research with marginalised groups where many of the proposed participants shy away when approached because they have other priorities. Time too is always a limiting factor and inevitably the majority of Traveller parents were reluctant to say too much to professionals, especially when they came from the settled community and were not seen to fully understand the ways and values of Traveller life.

This case story has investigated Traveller education through attempts to improve the access, attendance and school experiences of Traveller children. It illustrates how educational interventions which include parents can make a difference to school attendance and parental attitudes, and thus increase educational inclusion.

8. Teachers' inclusion strategies

For the past fifteen years Mike has been teaching in his present secondary school and during this time he has been involved with Traveller pupils. He has become more closely involved with them since he became a SENCO though he has always had between one and three Travellers in his class. Presently there are nine Traveller pupils on the school roll, in year 8, 9 and 11. It is of concern to Mike that Traveller children become the responsibility of the SENCO, who is primarily responsible for organising their individual learning needs. Until recently not much thinking or planning has gone into meeting the needs of these pupils through the school curriculum. They were seen as here today-gone-tomorrow, but this year there has been a push by the LEA to encourage these pupils to improve their attendance records. This means that teachers will have to make concerted efforts to provide curricula relevant to Traveller pupils' educational needs. Not only are the LEA taking an interest but they have just established a permanent maintained site for twenty families in the area.

To develop his investigation Mike used interviews, policy documents and general questioning in telephone calls to investigate who co-ordinates and takes responsibility for the education of Traveller children. Some of the questions to be answered are:

- does the LEA have a policy for the education of Traveller children?

- if yes, how is it to be implemented and by whom?

- does the school have a policy for the education of Traveller children?

- are the Traveller parents interested in improving their children's attendance and is the LEA in contact with parents?

Mike wanted to establish an overall picture of the situation to clarify his own thoughts, opinions, attitudes and to make him more understanding and informed about the schooling of Traveller children and young people. When he began the research on this topic he discovered how misinformed he was about the term itinerant. He thought itinerant, rather than Gypsy, was the term that Traveller children liked to use. He has subsequently discovered that Travellers is their preferred term of reference.

He began his research with a telephone call to the local Traveller support group and was fortunate to speak directly with its co-ordinator. The co-ordinator explained that an EWO had been appointed locally to work with Traveller children, and also as a liaison officer to support the schools that had Traveller pupils on roll. The co-ordinator believed that Travellers in the area were getting additional help because of a multi-agency government project which had just begun. He felt that the LEA seemed to be leading the way with the provision of pre-school facilities and the appointment of a new liaison officer allowed the EWO to spend more time with Traveller families and encourage school attendance. He hoped a youth and community worker would be appointed to the new official local Traveller site.

Although a comprehensive programme of education was one of the TESS current aims they were concentrating on immediate implementation of serviced sites throughout the region in the locations where Travellers had traditionally camped. It was felt that the shortage of settled places for Travellers to stay was a major impediment to regular schooling for their children.

Interviews with key personnel confirmed that education was regarded as a tool for providing a programme relevant to Traveller culture and would give them the opportunity to make their own decisions about future lifestyles.

Mike felt after his interviews with key LEA personnel that he knew who he could contact about Traveller support outside the school in the coming school year. At Mike's invitation the new liaison officer, Jan, paid a visit to the school and Mike was asked by the headteacher to co-ordinate all arrangements, timetabling and transport. The first meeting was taken up with establishing which Traveller pupils would be attending that school term and year, how Jan could best help and work together with him. They decided to work on a school policy for the education of Traveller pupils. This positive development differed from former years when teachers rarely catered for Traveller children's individual needs. Usually, most felt this was a futile exercise, as often the pupils left the school after a few days or weeks.

As a result of the initial meeting a drive was planned for intensive support for those pupils still not able to read proficiently. Five boys were selected for intensive learning support. These boys were in an illegal park in the area and were not yet attending the school because they had no school uniforms. Jan agreed to visit the school regularly every Wednesday and sort out issues related to late-coming, uniforms, attendance, books and co-operation with teachers. She was to be the vital link between parents and teachers.

After a number of meetings and discussions with Jan, Mike found that Traveller parents were willing to support their children's education in every way. Jan maintained her role as a support for their practical needs like uniform and transport to enable them to access the school. Jan and Mike together searched for and found additional curriculum materials to support the Traveller pupils' reading development, because the current reading material in school was unsuitable.

It was also negotiated and agreed after a number of trial sessions of shared teaching that Jan would contribute to specific teaching sessions that included Traveller pupils because of her positive rapport with them and their families. She would offer direct but limited support to pupils in the classroom. She was to help with reading, interpreting instructions and encouraging the pupils to participate fully in lessons. It was an experiment in co-operative teaching as an alternative to withdrawal teaching.

Jan initially supported a number of pupils in science classes, but the science teacher requested that the pupils be withdrawn rather than supported in class. As a consequence of discussions with headteacher it was agreed that Jan withdraw some pupils for intensive basic reading and numeracy lessons using materials devised by local Traveller associations. She continued to do this for short periods with Traveller pupils before re-integrating them into mainstream classes for science and other subjects. Regular staff meetings in school confirm that this experiment is working well and with Jan present at regular weekly sessions, mainstream teachers report fewer problems thanks to the additional support.

Mike found when he investigated his own teaching programme that he spent little time teaching individual Traveller pupils, and that his approach was very formal and desk based. So he has negotiated some time to develop active learning approaches in the school which will include Traveller pupils. He approached staff generally about his ideas, based on evidence that the classroom failure of specific pupils was related to sedentary and desk bound teaching activities. He showed how some Travellers' learning problems were linked to teaching approaches and learning style. He presented evidence from classroom observations, and feedback from Traveller pupils after specific lessons. He linked their successful (or otherwise) learning to teaching styles and individual pupils' active interactions. Traveller pupils are accustomed to active and interactive learning in a natural setting and much of the teaching in school was too desk bound for them. With the support of senior management and colleagues, Mike arranged a programme of outside visits to places of educational interest in the Autumn term, because Traveller pupils would be more likely to be on roll at that time of year. He wanted the active learning programme in school to be inclusive, so he randomly selected pupils from year groups which also included Travellers. With the support of colleagues, he planned to introduce more active teaching and learning to all subjects and to encourage Traveller pupils to negotiate and agree to minimal attendance each week. This has been accepted for the first term of the new school year. The only thing left now is the further collection of evidence to evaluate the success or otherwise of the initiative with all pupils including Traveller pupils.

So far this initiative has shown the attendance of Traveller pupils has markedly increased by thirty per cent and one parent said of her teenage boys that 'They used to be afraid of school but now they go more easily'. The school staff are meeting regularly with the aim of formulating a Traveller school policy based on the principles of Traveller pupils:

- feeling secure and happy

- being more willing to attend school

- being able to approach school staff with problems

- feeling able to trust their teachers and carers

- developing trusting relationships to ensure that the learning process in school is productive.

The school is creating individualised learning programmes for all Traveller pupils who attend. Arrangements have been made for these programmes to be sent ahead to their new schools or Traveller education advisors when they travel. Although intensive basic programmes continue to be put in place for individual pupils, their inclusion in mainstream classes has been eased by the progress Traveller pupils have made with this additional help. Support assistants and teachers already employed by the LEA are aware that it is important to ensure that Traveller pupils do not become identified as pupils with special educational needs. All additional support is now undertaken in Traveller only groups, away from the main classroom, for at least one hour each day. Traveller pupils then spend the rest of each day with general support in mainstream lessons. It is proving to be a very successful means of making sure they are not seen to be too special and can progress with pre-organised and prepared worksheets and programmes negotiated with individual subject teachers. The research has found that there are no specific policies or programmes for Travellers in the area other than those being presently created and enacted. It is expected that next year they will be adopted formally as policy documents in the LEA and its schools.

Parents are visited regularly by Louise and school attendance has increased. New pre-school initiatives, better travel arrangements for children attending nurseries and schools, and an understanding that more is being done to support the learning of secondary age Traveller pupils have increased Traveller families' confidence about the benefits of education.

Mike and his school colleagues meet with Jan each week to discuss any problems or areas of pupil and school progress. Teachers and other staff have been persuaded not to see the education of Traveller pupils as the role of the SENCO but as a whole school responsibility. And local multi-agency co-operation for the benefit of Travellers is being firmly established through involvement in these new school initiatives.

References

Acton T, Marselos J, Szego P (2000) *Language, Blacks and Gypsies*, Acton T and Dalphinis A (eds), London: Whiting and Birch

Anisha B (1997) *The Declaration of a Lost People*. Wolverhampton: WMCESTC

Aristotle (1977) *The Politics*, trans H Rackham. London: Heinemann.

Association of Teachers of Language (ATL) (1999) *Balancing Acts*. Report, London: 20 (5)

Banks JA (1989) Multicultural education: characteristics and goals, in Banks J.A., McGee Banks C.A (eds) *Multicultural Education: Issues and Perspectives*. Massachusetts, Allyn and Bacon

Bell J (1993) *Doing Your Own Research Project*. Buckingham: Open University Press

Brandt G L (1986) *The Realisation of Anti-Racist Teaching*. East Sussex: Falmer Press

Brown B (1998) *Unlearning Discrimination in the Early Years*. Staffordshire: Trentham Books

Bullivant BM (1989) Culture: Its Nature and Meaning for Educators, in Banks JA McGee Banks CA (eds) *op.cit.*

Clarke C (1998) *A Step Change in Traveller Education*. Speech to NATT. London: DfEE

Commission of European Communities (1989) The Ministries of Education meeting with the Council 22nd May 1989 on *School Provision for Children of Occupational Travellers (Fairground, Circus, Bargee)*. Luxembourg EEC

Davis G (1986) Strategies for change, in Arora R, Duncan C *Multicultural Education: Towards Good Practice*. London: Routledge and Kegan Paul

Department of Health (1989) *Working together under the Children Act*, London: HMSO

Department of Education and Science (1980) *The Education of Gypsy, Fairground and Circus Children and Others Who Lead Nomadic Lives*. London: DES

Department of Education and Science (1985) *Education for All (Swann Report)*, London: DES

Department of Education and Science (1989) *Children Act*. London: HMSO

Department of Education and Science (1990) *DES Circular 10/90 Education Reform Act 1988: Specific Grant for the Education of Travellers and Displaced Persons. Section 210.* London: DES

Department of Education and Science (1992) *Curriculum Organisation and Classroom Practice in Primary School.* London: DES

Department of Health (1998) Health Service Circular 1998/229. London: DoH

DETR and Home Office (1998) *Managing Unauthorised Camping. A good practice guide.* London: DfEE

Department for Education and Employment (1994) *School Attendance: Policy and Practice on Categorisation of Absence.* London: DfEE

DfEE (1997) *Excellence in Schools.* London: DfEE

DfEE (1998) *Making the Difference: Teaching and Learning Strategies in Successful Multi-ethnic Schools.* London: DfEE

DfEE (1998) *National Literacy Strategy.* London: DfEE

DfEE (1998) Are We Missing Out? Video. London: DfEE

DfES (2001) Are We Missing Out (video for parents) London: DfES

DfES (2003) *Schools admissions Code of Practice.* London: DfES

DfES (2003) *Aiming High,* consultation document. London: DfES

EU (1989) *School Provision for Gypsy and Traveller Children.* Council Resolution. Brussels: EU

Elliott J (1981) *Action Research for Educational Change.* Buckingham: Open University Press.

Gay G (1989) Ethnic minorities and educational equality in Banks JA, McGee Banks CA (eds) *op.cit.*

Grant CA and Sleeter CE (1989) Race, Class, Gender: Exceptionality and Educational Reform in Banks JA McGee Banks CA (eds) *op.cit.*

Grundy S (1982) Three Modes of Action Research. *Curriculum Perspectives* 2, (3)

Habermas J (1986) *The Theory of Communicative Action, vol 1 Reason and the rationalisation of Society.* Cambridge: Polity Press

HMSO (1960) *Caravan Sites and Control of Development Act.* London: HMSO

HMSO (1966) *The Education Act.* London: HMSO

HMSO (1985) *The Housing Act.* London: HMSO

HMSO (1987) *Gypsies and Travellers: Public Order Act.* London: HMSO

HMSO (1994) *The UK's first Report to the UN Committee on the Rights of the Child.* London: HMSO

HMSO (1994) *The Criminal Justice and Public Order Act.* London: HMSO

HMSO (1998) *The Human Rights Act.* London: HMSO

HMSO (2000) *Race Relations (Amendment) Act.* London: HMSO

Holly ML (1989) Reflective Writing and the Spirit of Inquiry, *Cambridge Journal of Education.* 19 (1)

Holmes P (1993) Traveller Education; Structural response to Cultural Diversity, in Fyfe A and Figueroa P (eds), *Education for Cultural Diversity. The challenge for a new era.* London: Routledge

Holmes P and Jordan E (1997) The Interrupted Learner – whose responsibility? in Bastiani J (ed) *Home-School Work in Multicultural settings.* London: David Fulton

Home Office (1994) *Criminal Justice and Public Order Act* 1994, Circular 45/1994. London: HMSO

Holmes P, Knaepkens L and Marks D (2000). *Fighting Social Exclusion through ODL.* Lisbon EEC

Ivatts A (1998) *Afterword in School Provision for Ethnic Minorities: The Gypsy Paradigm.* Hatfield: University of Hertfordshire Press

Ivatts A (1999) *Why include the Gypsies in IEP: Meeting the Individual Needs of Children from Minority Ethnic Groups.* London: Intercultural Education Partnership

Kenrick D and Clark C (1995) *Moving On, The Gypsies and Travellers of Britain.* Hatfield: University of Hertfordshire Press

Kiddle C (1999) *Traveller Children: a Voice for Themselves.* London: Jessica Kingsley

Liegeois JP (1998) *School Provision for Ethnic Minorities: The Gypsy Paradigm.* Hatfield: University of Hertfordshire Press

MacAlister RS (1937) *The Secret Languages of Ireland.* Cambridge: Cambridge University Press

Macpherson W *et al* (1999) *The Stephen Lawrence Inquiry Report.* London: HMSO

Marsh M (1999) Melting Pot is not enough. London: *Times Educational Supplement* 12th March

National Gypsy Council Report (undated), *Discrimination.* London: National Gypsy Council

Morris R and Clements L (eds) (1999) *Gaining Ground; law reform for Gypsies and Travellers.* Hatfield: University of Hertfordshire

NATT (1998) *Exclusion and Truancy.* Wolverhampton: National Association for Teachers of Travellers

Naylor T and Wild-Smith S (1997) *Broadening Horizons.* Chelmsford: Essex County Council

Ofsted (1995) *Guidance on the Inspection of Nursery and Primary Schools.* London: HMSO

Ofsted (1995) *Guidance on the Inspection of Nursery and Primary Schools.* London: HMSO

Ofsted (1996) *The Education of Travelling Children.* London: Ofsted

Ofsted (1999) *Raising the Attainment of Minority Ethnic Pupils.* London: Ofsted

Ofsted (2000) *Inspecting Subjects 3-11.* London: Ofsted

Ofsted (2000) *LEA Support for School Improvement: Framework for the Inspection of Local Education Authorities.* London: Ofsted

Ofsted (2001) *Managing Support for the Attainment of Pupils from Ethnic Minority Groups.* London: Ofsted

O'Hanlon (1993) The Importance of an articulated Personal Theory of Professional Development, in *Reconstructing Teacher Education*, J Elliott (ed). London: Falmer Press

O'Hanlon C (1995) Why is action research a valid basis for professional development? in, Mc Bride R (ed) *Teacher Education Policy: some issues arising from research and practice.* London: Falmer Press

O'Hanlon C (1996) *What is Your School doing For Travelling Children?* Staff Development Pack. Brussels: EFECOT

O'Hanlon C (1997) The professional journal as a pedagogical basis for personal and professional in higher education, in Hollingsworth S (ed) (1997) *International Action Research: a Casebook for Educational Reform,* London: Falmer Press

O'Hanlon C (1999) *An Introduction to Action Research.* Course hand-out. Norwich University of East Anglia

O'Hanlon C (2003) *Educational Inclusion as Action research; an interpretive discourse.* Buckingham: Open University Press

Pahl J and Vaile M (1986) *Health and Health Care among Travellers.* Canterbury: University of Kent

Phillips S (1994) Managing young children's behaviour, in Abbott L, and Roger R (eds) *Quality Education in the Early Years.* Buckingham: Open University Press

Rigby R (1998) *First Steps Developmental Continuum.* Education Department of Western Australia. London: Heinemann

Royal College of Physicians (1988) Health Service Circular 1998/229. Faculty of Public Health Medicine. London: University of London

Teacher Training Agency (1998) *National Standards for Qualified Teacher Status.* London: TTA

Troyna B (1993) *Racism and Education.* Buckingham: Open University Press

West Midlands Consortium Education Service for Travelling Children (1993) *What is your school doing for Travelling Children? A guide to equal opportunities through Distance Learning.* Brussels: EFECOT

West Midlands Consortium Education Service for Travelling Children (1995) *Moving Targets, a Handbook for Service Providers.* WMCESTC. Wolverhampton: Steering Group for Travellers

Worcester CC (2001) *You Don't Know Me: Gypsies and Travellers resident on Worcester CC Sites.* Wychaven District Council: The Rural Media Company

Zeichner K (1993) Action Research: personal renewal and social reconstruction, *Educational Action Research Journal* 1 (2).

Appendix I

Key education policy documents on raising the attainment of Gypsy and Traveller pupils

The main findings from key education policy are outlined as follows:

1. The Education of Travelling Children, Ofsted 1996

This is an HMI Report. More than 31 LEAs were visited for inspection between September 1992 and July 1995. The findings were as follows:

- The number of Traveller children 0-16 years 'may be as large as 50,000'. This represents a significant advance on earlier estimates

- The administration of funding for Traveller Education is efficient and effective. The grant represents good value for money

- Considerable progress has been made in the development of positive attitudes and trusting relationships between schools and the different travelling communities who, by reason of their nomadic lifestyle, have traditionally been hindered in their access to education

- Over England as a whole, access to school is significantly more secure for Travelling children of primary age and there is evidence to suggest that although there are below average levels of participation at the pre school level, the situation is slowly improving

- Access to the curriculum for secondary aged children remains a matter of grave concern. There are probably as many as 10,000 children at this phase who are not even registered with a school

- The attendance at school of Travelling children is slowly improving, but the average figures are still unacceptably low

- There is no separate systematic and unified recording of the standards of achievement by Travelling pupils. However, standards of achievement based on inspection evidence are satisfactory for Travelling pupils in the early years. Standards for pupils at KS1 and 2 are generally improving, although there is serious and legitimate concern for some groups, despite an earlier start at school and more regular attendance, standards of achievement, particularly in English, are disappointing. Standards of achievement at the secondary phase are variable, but on the whole unsatisfactory

• The work of Traveller Education Services (TES) is generally of a high standard. Staffing and other resources are well managed and deployed and are generally very effective within the constraints imposed by the current level of funding

• The quality of teaching and other welfare support is generally good and out-standingly so in a significant number of projects

• A disproportionate number of Travelling pupils, particularly at the secondary phase, are excluded from school. This is despite the general assessment that the behaviour of Travelling pupils is good

• The number of Travelling young people who have access to and take advantage of post school vocational training and further and higher education is worry-ingly small.

2. Raising the attainment of minority ethnic pupils: school and LEA responses (Ofsted 1999)

For this report a sample of 48 schools were selected because of the percentage of pupils from each of the four focus groups – Bangladeshi, Black Caribbean, Pakistan, Gypsy Traveller.

Gypsy Traveller Pupils

• None of the primary schools were carrying out systematic monitoring of attainment by ethnicity.

However, it is clear that Gypsy Traveller pupils achieve less well on average than other pupils in their school. In two schools there was serious evidence of under-achievement. In one of these, Gypsy Traveller children formed 18% of the school roll but represented 50% of the statemented pupils – over half the Gypsy Traveller pupils were on the SEN register.

In the second school, 74% of Gypsy Traveller pupils were on the SEN register.

• At the point of transfer to secondary schools, Gypsy Traveller attainment is well below school and national averages. This results in the majority being placed on school SEN registers. In all schools where the information was avail-able, over 50% of the Gypsy Traveller population were on the SEN register. In half the schools, no Gypsy Traveller child has yet sat for GCSE

• Of the four focus groups in this survey, Gypsy Traveller children are the most at risk in the education system. Although some make a reasonably promising start in primary school, by the time they reach secondary school their levels of attainment are almost always a matter for concern. Many, especially boys, opt out of education by Year 9 and very few go on to achieve success at GCSE or beyond.

The report continues:

• *The collection and use of attainment data.* All the Gypsy Traveller Primary schools supplied their LEA with National Curriculum information for Gypsy Traveller children.

- *Teaching strategies.* Teacher expectations of Gypsy Traveller pupils are generally unreasonably low. This is true even where policies in some schools to raise expectations and attainment for all children are generally effective....

- Raising the expectation of Gypsy Traveller pupils among secondary teachers is probably the most urgent priority. Many arrive at secondary school with depressed reading scores and the fact that such a high proportion feature on SEN registers tends to reinforce the view of them as low achievers. Although several headteachers were quite explicit about this general concern to raise teacher expectation, and whole school and departmental target setting were important aspects of this, only one school had specific targets for the achievement of Gypsy Traveller pupils.

- *Staff responsibilities and use of additional grant.* All of the Gypsy Traveller primary schools benefit from additional teaching and ancillary support provided by Traveller Education Services... Where Gypsy Traveller pupils are valued in the same way as other pupils the support of the TES is welcomed and embraced in a way which leads to effective and well co-ordinated provision.

- There is a tendency in some schools to see the TES as responsible for the Gypsy Traveller pupils and as go between with the parents, rather than the school itself. The reluctance to accept full responsibility for the children goes against the development of co-ordinated action to improve the attendance and raise levels of attainment.

- All the Gypsy Traveller secondary schools receive some additional funding to help support the needs of their Gypsy Traveller pupils. This amounts to two days part time work by a teacher from the local TES, shared access to Home School liaison/ and Education Welfare Officers.

- Traveller Education Service job description is broad. Links with Special Educational Needs co-ordinators runs risk of stereotyping all Travellers as low attainers.

- Curriculum Review. Wide ranges of responses across curriculum in the inclusion of Gypsy Travellers issues, concerns, history and so forth.

- Strategies aimed at Gypsies and Travellers, Medical Appointment's, support for pupil visits and TES informal mentor.

- Pastoral needs recognised, some good practice developing recognising hostility and racism stereotyping; flexible approaches to school rules and procedures demonstrated without compromising school policies.

- Transfer strategies are outlined. Support for Key Stage 4 attendance to encourage staying on.

- Guidelines to staff as way of keeping pupils in contact with formal learning through temporary part-time timetables; collaboration between school, parents, child, TES and EWOs.

- Attendance at schools; considerable effort was put into encouraging good attendance and punctuality. Supported by EWO.

Promoting high rates of attendance

- TES regularly monitor attendance and follow up in recognition that if not in regular attendance school academic programme will be seriously affected. Retention beyond Year 9, absence at critical points of year such as SATs were problematic. One school demonstrated that it is not inevitable that the pupils will be poor attenders.

- *Promoting good standards of behaviour.* Schools had detailed knowledge of excluded pupils and could report to LEA and TES re Gypsy Travellers. Permanent exclusion is rare in these schools. No Gypsy or Traveller child excluded that year 1996/1997.

- Additional support at lunchtime for Gypsy Traveller pupils has proved helpful.

- *Study support.* Gypsy and Traveller children had negligible involvement in extra curricular activities and only one school fully appreciated the social and educational importance of ensuring Gypsy Travellers are encouraged to participate as fully as possible. School is aware of practical and racial factors militating against inclusion in after school activities and both staff and TES personnel provide transport home after events where appropriate.

  Links with parents. The involvement of Gypsy Traveller parents in the life and work of primary school presents particular challenges. Home visits, support for form filling, reading letters and official documents, assisting with benefit entitlements will all increase involvement. Ones school provides transport for parents to school events and parents evenings. Level of participation by Gypsy Traveller parents reported to be disappointing.

- Overall relatively few of the secondary schools have systematic and coherent strategies for improving the quality of relationships between home and school.

- Several of the secondary schools with Gypsy Traveller parents have worked hard to build up good relationships. The help of TES was felt to have been a 'crucial factor' in gaining confidence of families. It has taken a long time to build links and schools comment these often remain fragile – misunderstandings can easily arise causing setbacks. For this reason, individual contact is essential. Where senior members of staff take time to visit the sites in addition to TES teachers, Travellers spoke warmly of the school and its support for them.

- *Links with the wider community.* In connection with the Gypsy Traveller community, one school commented that it had difficulty in knowing how to deal with a community that had no obvious infrastructure, no recognised centre and no clear community leaders.

- *Promoting good race relations.* All the Gypsy Traveller schools report considerable local prejudice with children usually following example of parents. Indeed the level of hostility faced by Gypsy and Traveller children is probably greater than for any other minority ethnic group. Headteachers had no doubt that the extended hostility impacts on life of the school. Consciousness of the racist prejudice within the local community acts as a hindrance in some schools to more fully embracing the Gypsy Traveller community into life and work of school including the necessary development of the curriculum for all pupils.

- TES staff promote good self image for Gypsy Traveller pupils but to have any lasting effect this needs to be encouraged and supported at whole school level.

  One secondary school has effective strategies in developing confidence and pride so that pupils do not feel the need to hide their Traveller identity as is the case in some schools.

- In one school TES staff encouraged Gypsy Traveller pupils to produce booklets and other material to promote the positives side of the culture. This led to greater understanding at peer group level.

3. Managing Support for the Attainment of Pupils from Minority Ethnic Groups Ofsted 2001.

The report is based on the inspection of 21 Traveller Education Services and short visits to nine other services between 1999 and 2001.

Chapter 4 – Traveller education: Management of support in LEAs and schools

- Traveller Education Services were invariably judged to be satisfactory or better with a number of very good services.

- Monitoring of Gypsy Traveller pupils achievement by LEA services showed some marked improvement. However, there was still a serious concern in the secondary phase about access, attendance and achievement.

- TES were very well managed in terms of support to schools and Traveller pupils and provided good value for money. The majority of TES are managed by experienced and well informed teacher co-ordinators.

- Line management of TES within LEAs varied in quality and effectiveness but was generally good. The status and experience of many services was enhanced by inclusion within Education Development Plans. A surprising number of plans made no such reference reflecting in a few cases less than adequate knowledge of and attention to the TES on the part of senior LEA managers.

- The management of additional teaching and other resources within the school was good although generally more emphasis was placed on individual pupil support than whole school action. Best practice was based on agreement and the focus of support, time limits and review dates for individual pupils.

- Another feature was the commitment by the school to arrange cultural awareness raising training for some or all staff including setting support for Traveller education in the context of equal opportunities and race equality.

- Among the LEAs, service management at its best was dynamic and creative. Teams were well supported. Centrally managed services were flexible and able to meet changing needs and circumstances.

- Pupil support by TES staff was frequently effective but liaison with class teachers was not always thorough, and their knowledge of roles and the expectation of the service staff was sometimes ill defined. The quality of teaching and learning was better when there were well established routines for joint planning, teaching and evaluation.

- Schools benefited significantly where time was devoted to joint planning and teaching about Gypsy Traveller culture and history. This improved knowledge and understanding of all pupils in the class and increased self esteem of Gypsy Traveller pupils and improved their attainment. Schools relied heavily on TES to provide books and materials and there was some reluctance on the part of schools to purchase materials for themselves.

- All successful work securing regular attendance and confident and successful learning was directly linked to the quality of the relationship with the parents. Mutual respect and trust are essential to these relationships. The best practice which was not uniform, was characterised by services helping the schools to develop these relationships and by not usurping the schools' duties and responsibilities by retaining the go between role.

- For a significant proportion of pupils from Gypsy Traveller families, educational discontinuity was a major factor to under achievement. Within the constraints of resources all services attempted to provide support to schools with pupils from Traveller families with predictable patterns of migration in the preparation of distance learning materials. These travelled with pupils and units of completed work were exchanged with schools for new work packs.

- Children entering other schools as the travelled carried an educational record which was maintained by pupil, TES or schools. TES have usually initiated distance learning sometimes jointly with the base school, although some schools were less than willing or able to play a full part.

- Most TES had inspired interagency action within their local authority area or region. Where such senior managers were involved in these developments they had helped to secure better co-ordination of policy and practice in relation to the different transient and nomadic communities.

- Many services had education welfare officers or social workers designated as education liaison workers. Duties varied, but essentially included establishing relationships with families, identification of schools places, encouraging regular attendance. Work with mobile groups, despite sometimes poor levels of attendance, was usually of a good standard. There were some management difficulties of these posts as a result of differences between responsibilities and approaches of postholders and those teachers and learning support assistants within TES.

Broader Issues

- Issues of access and attendance at school combine to bring a large number of TES into conflict with schools, other LEA departments and national policies.

- Many of the Traveller sites are at a distance from schools or on marginal land which represents major environmental and health dangers to residents. Home to school transport is frequently required and helpfully provided even where the distance is below statutory minimum above which free transport must be provided. However, decisions taken by some LEAs not to use their discretionary powers have militated against better attendance. It is important that decisions are based on objective factors and are taken in the light of the need to maximise attendance at school.

- Most TES had lists of pupils known not to be registered in any school or registered but seldom attending. In the majority of services, action was being pursued in relation to individual children. However, in many cases, action was not being taken or was inadequate with mainstream education welfare services failing to take direct responsibility. There was a general and disappointing tendency for these services to see the attendance and welfare of Traveller children as the exclusive responsibility of the TES.

- In all LEAs inspected, Traveller families moved to the area temporarily. Because of shortage of designated sites families stopped on land not authorised for the purpose. Where through effective interagency group work good working relationships had been established between the TES and the relevant department, early notification resulted in rapid outreach to such families and the initial securing of appropriate school places. However, positive efforts by the TES to fulfil the LEAs statutory responsibilities were sometimes at odds with the practice in the eviction of the families. In a number of cases decisions taken by authorities appeared not to take into account adequately the educational and other needs of the children in these circumstances.

- In a few schools in a small number of LEAs inspected, reservations had been expressed about taking on pupils from Traveller families; such schools clearly failing to recognise their legal responsibilities.

  There was a growing trend in about half of the LEAs inspected for Traveller families to opt for education at home particularly in the secondary phase. Services responded with appropriate advice but the practice on registration and monitoring varied significantly among LEAs. The lack of evaluative monitoring typified the poorest provision.

Recommendations

- At the national level:

  - More systematic development and use of distance learning materials

  - Fuller guidance to LEAs on policy and practice in relation to education at home as it affects Traveller children.

- LEAs and TES should ensure that:

  - The use of peripatetic staff to support schools is defined by a service agreement covering roles, functions and classroom practice as well as the means by which whole school briefing is given on the support and the background of pupils

  - There is closer connection between Traveller education services and LEA inspectors and advisers.

  - More schools are made aware of the need to develop relationships with Traveller parents to take account of the cultural background of their children and to provide appropriate curriculum resources.

  - LEA judgement on the provision of home to school transport for Travellers are based on objective factors including risk analysis and the need to promote regular attendance at school.

- LEA education welfare services carry out their responsibilities for all children in their areas including Traveller children not registered with schools or only residing temporarily either in authorised or un-authorised sites, in order to address high levels of non attendance among pupils from Traveller families of secondary age.

- Decisions on the eviction of Traveller families have regard to the statutory duties of LEAs on the provision of education.

- These steps in relation to the use of the grant need to be matched in LEAs and schools by continuing wider efforts to improve policy and practice with regard to ethnic minority achievement and race equality It is essential to ensure that action is taken to meet the recommendations of the Stephen Lawrence Inquiry report.

Appendix 2

Useful Addresses

National Association of Teachers of Travellers (NATT)
Aims to reduce the professional isolation of teachers of Travellers and provide a voice for improving services to Travellers and to seek improvement in the education and vocational training opportunities for Gypsy and Traveller children and their families. Founder member of European Federation for the Education of Children of Occupational Travellers (EFECOT).

Central address
C/o WMCESTC
The Graiseley Centre, Pool Street
Wolverhampton WV2 4NE
Tel: 01902 714646

The European Federation for the Education of Children of Occupational Travellers (EFECOT)
Aims to promote the education of Gypsy and Traveller, Fairground and Circus and Bargee children and their families through extensive networks and project development and activity. Director: Ludo Knaepkens

Vooruitgangstraat 333/2
Rue de Progres 333/2, B1030 Brussels
Tel: 0032 2 2274060
Fax: 0032 2 2274069
e-mail: efecot@efecot.net
www.efecot.net

Centre de Recherche Tsiganes
Publishes Interface providing information across member states, networking opportunities, research and writing projects. Director: Jean Pierre Liegeois

Centre de Recherche Tsiganes
Universite de Paris, 106 Quai de Clichy,
F92110 CLICHY, France

Appendix 3

Resources

The following Traveller Education Services produce culture specific teaching and learning materials for sale:

Avon Consortium Traveller Education Service
Charborough Road, Filton, Bristol, BS34 7R
Tel: 01454 862620/21 Fax: 01454 862619
e-mail lynda_howells@southglos.gov.uk

Bolton Education Service for Showmen and Travellers BESST
Castle Hill Resource Centre, Castleton Street, Bolton BL2 2JW
Tel: 01204 338150 Fax: 01204 338151
e-mail travellers.education@bolton.gov.uk

Cheshire Traveller Education Service
The Professional Centre, Woodford Lodge, Woodford Lane West, Winsford CW7 4EH
Tel: 01606 814330 Fax: 01606 860160
e-mail walker/@cheshire.gov.uk

Devon Consortium Traveller Education Service
Southern Division Office, Redworth House, Ashburton Road, Totnes, Devon, TQ9 5JZ
Tel: 01392 386 811 Fax: 01392 386 829
e-mail maxford@devon.gov.uk www.devon.gov.uk/eal/traveller

Durham and Darlington Traveller Education Service
Broom Cottages Primary School, Broom Cottages, Ferryhill, DL17 8AN
Tel: 01740 656998 Fax: 01740 657792
e-mail angela.tierney@durham.gov.uk

Essex and Southend Consortium Traveller Education Service
C/o Alec Hunter High School, Stubbs Lane, Braintree CM7 3NT
Tel: 01376 340360 Fax: 01376 340360
e-mail jackie.nesbitt@essex.gov.uk
www.essexcc.gov.uk

Haringey Traveller Education Service
Haringey Professional Development Centre
Downhills, Park Road, London N17 6AR
Tel: 020 8489 5069 Fax: 0208489 5004
e-mail judy.bohan@haringey.gov.uk
judy.bohan@binternet.com

Kent Traveller Education Service
Minority Communities Achievement Service
Kent CC, Invicta House, 3rd floor County Hall, Maidstone ME14 1XX
Tel: 01622 694207 Fax: 01622 694971
e-mail lynda.reeves@kent.gov.uk

Lancashire Traveller Education Consortium
8 East Cliff, Preston, PR1 3JE
Tel:01772 263 826 Fax: 01772 262 737
e-mail jeanne.kenyon@ed.lancscc.gov.uk

Leicestershire Traveller Education Service
Bennet Centre, Beaumanor Park, Woodhouse, Leicester LE12 8TX
Tel: 01509 890546 Fax: 01509 891414
e-mail mhutchinson@leics.gov.uk

Newham Traveller Education Service
Credon Centre, Kirton Road, Plaistow London E13 9BT
Tel: 0208430 6279 Fax: 020 8430 6279
e-mail anthea.wormington@newham.gov.uk
andrew.delamere@newham.gov.uk

Norfolk Traveller Education Service
Traveller Resource Base, Turner Road, Norwich NR2 4HB
Tel: 01603 766133 Fax: 01603 767315
e-mail norftrav.educ@btinternet.com
lorna.daymon.edu@norfolk.gov.uk

Suffolk Traveller Education Centre
Multicultural Office, SSPDC, Pauls Road, Ipswich IP2 0AN
Tel: 01473 583 530 Fax: 01473 583 531
Mobile: 0771 769654
e-mail timeverson@educ.suffolkcc.gov.uk

Wiltshire Traveller Education Service
East Wing, County Hall, Bythesea Road, Trowbridge BA14 8JQ
Tel: 01225 771687 Fax: 01225 771681
e-mail kathrynyeaman@wiltshire.gov.uk

West Midlands Consortium Education Service for Travelling Children
WMCESTC, The Graiseley Centre, Pool Street, Wolverhampton WV2 4NE
Tel: 01902 714646 Fax: 01902 714202
e-mail wmcestc@dial.pipex.com

NATT
C/o WMCESTC, The Graiseley Centre, Pool St., Wolverhampton WV2 4NE
Tel: 01902 714646 Fax: 01902 714202
e-mail wmcestc@dial.pipex.com

The Smiths Secondary Literacy Programme
Circus Spotlight (Photographs, Broadsheet and worksheet pack (8-11)
Parent Education Contact Book
Information Pack

DfES
Video 'Are We Missing Out' (secondary transfer)
DfES Publication Order Line
Tel: 0845 6022260 Fax: 0845 6033360

Showmen's Guild of Great Britain
Central Office, Guild House, 41 Clarence House, Staines, Middlesex, TW18 4SY
Tel: 01784 461805

On The Fair CD Rom

'Knockabouts' Wooden toys and jigsaws
Dave and Angela Knock
23 Wheatacres, Norfolk IP 24 1AQ.
Tel: 01842 762560

'Still Roamin' Handmade Furniture
18 Ramsey Close, Forest town, Mansfield, Notts. NG19 0NS
Tel: 01623 650512
e-mail stillroamin@lineone.net

The Parrotfish Company Wooden Toys
51 North Street, Maldon, Essex CM9 5HJ
Tel: 01621 858940 Fax: 01621 858940
e-mail enquiries@parrotfish.co.uk
www.parrotfish.co.uk

University of Hertfordshire Press
Publishers of Interface Collection
University of Hertfordshire
College Lane, Hatfield, Hertfordshire AL10 9AB
Tel: 1707 2846. Fax: 1707 284666

Index